DeepSeek-Vision Language for Developers: A Practical Approach to Multimodal AI

Francisco A. Collier

Preface

Artificial Intelligence has come a long way, and with the rise of **multimodal AI**, we are witnessing a new frontier—one where machines can **see, read, and understand the world much like humans do**. This shift is powered by **vision-language models (VLMs)**, which combine computer vision and natural language processing to create intelligent systems capable of understanding both text and images simultaneously.

Among these advancements, **DeepSeek-VL** has emerged as a powerful open-source model, offering **cutting-edge multimodal capabilities** with accessibility for developers and researchers alike. Whether you want to build an **AI-powered search engine**, an **intelligent chatbot that understands images**, or **automate content generation**, DeepSeek-VL provides a solid foundation. But how do you actually implement it? How can you leverage its capabilities to solve real-world problems? That's exactly what this book aims to teach you.

Who Is This Book For?

This book is written for **developers, AI enthusiasts, and researchers** who want to understand and implement **DeepSeek-VL** in practical applications. If you're new to multimodal AI, don't worry—I'll guide you through the basics. If you're an experienced machine learning engineer, you'll find advanced topics like **fine-tuning, custom dataset integration, and deployment** that will help you push the boundaries of what DeepSeek-VL can do.

By the end of this book, you'll be able to:
Understand the **core concepts** of vision-language AI.
Set up and run **DeepSeek-VL** for various tasks like **image captioning, visual question answering (VQA), and text-to-image retrieval**.
Fine-tune DeepSeek-VL for your **own datasets and applications**.
Deploy DeepSeek-VL **at scale**, optimizing it for real-world use cases.

How This Book Is Structured

I believe in a **hands-on, step-by-step approach** to learning. That's why this book is structured as a **progressive guide**, starting with foundational concepts and moving towards advanced implementations.

- **Part 1: Foundations of Vision-Language AI** introduces the **fundamentals of multimodal AI** and the architecture of DeepSeek-VL.
- **Part 2: Getting Started with DeepSeek-VL** walks you through **installation, API usage, and basic implementations**.
- **Part 3: Building and Customizing Models** explores **fine-tuning, dataset preparation, and scaling DeepSeek-VL for production**.
- **Part 4: Advanced Topics and Future Trends** dives into **cutting-edge applications, ethical considerations, and where vision-language AI is headed**.

Each chapter includes **clear explanations, practical code examples, and real-world use cases** to make learning intuitive and engaging.

Why This Book?

There are plenty of resources on **vision-language models**, but most focus on **high-level theory or overly complex research papers**. This book bridges the gap—it's **technical but accessible, practical yet insightful**. It's written for **developers who want to build, not just understand**.

Let's Get Started!

If you're ready to unlock the full potential of **DeepSeek-VL** and create **intelligent multimodal AI applications**, let's dive in! Grab your keyboard, set up your development environment, and let's build something amazing together.

Table of Contents

DeepSeek-VL, like most vision-language models, is built on a powerful
architecture that allows it to process both images and text efficiently.................. 26

Part 1: Foundations of Vision-Language AI

Chapter 1: Introduction to DeepSeek-VL and Multimodal AI

Artificial Intelligence has come a long way, from simple rule-based systems to deep learning models capable of generating human-like text and recognizing objects in images. But today, AI is taking an even bigger leap— one that goes beyond just understanding text or images independently.

Welcome to the world of **multimodal AI**, where models can process and understand information across multiple data types—text, images, and even videos—just like we do. This evolution has given rise to powerful **vision-language models (VLMs)** like **DeepSeek-VL**, which bring a new level of intelligence to AI systems.

In this chapter, we'll explore **what multimodal AI is**, **how vision-language models have evolved**, **why DeepSeek-VL stands out**, and **where it is making an impact in the real world**.

1.1 What is Multimodal AI?

Artificial Intelligence has made incredible progress in recent years, with models that can understand and generate text, analyze images, and even process speech. But the real world isn't limited to just one type of data. Humans naturally process multiple modes of information simultaneously— we read text, interpret facial expressions, analyze visual scenes, and make sense of spoken words all at once. **Multimodal AI** is an effort to bring this kind of comprehensive understanding to machines.

At its core, multimodal AI refers to **systems that can process, understand, and generate content using multiple types of data—such as text, images, audio, and video—simultaneously.** Instead of treating each data type in isolation, these models combine different forms of information to create richer, more accurate interpretations.

Consider how we interact with the world. When looking at a photograph of a busy city street, we don't just see objects; we understand context. We recognize the presence of cars, people crossing the road, storefronts, and even the mood of the scene—perhaps a rainy evening with reflections of lights on the pavement. Now, imagine an AI model that can not only recognize the objects in the image but also describe the atmosphere, answer questions about the scene, or even generate a story based on it. That's the power of multimodal AI.

Breaking the Barriers of Unimodal AI

Traditional AI models have been largely **unimodal**, meaning they focus on one type of data at a time. A language model like GPT can generate text, while a computer vision model like ResNet can analyze images. But real-world applications often require an understanding that spans multiple modalities.

For example, a **medical AI assistant** should be able to process both **doctor's notes (text)** and **X-ray scans (images)** to provide accurate diagnoses. A **self-driving car** must interpret **camera feeds (vision)** and **spoken commands (audio)** to navigate safely. By integrating multiple modes of data, AI systems become significantly more powerful and context-aware.

One of the most impactful shifts in AI research over the last few years has been the development of **vision-language models (VLMs)**—a subset of multimodal AI that combines image and text understanding. These models, like **DeepSeek-VL**, can analyze pictures and generate natural language descriptions, answer questions about images, or even match visuals with the most relevant textual information.

How Multimodal AI Works

Multimodal AI models rely on architectures that can process and align different types of data effectively. This is typically achieved through **transformers**, a deep learning framework that has revolutionized AI by allowing models to understand complex relationships within and across data types.

A key challenge in multimodal AI is creating a **shared representation space**—a way for the model to interpret images, text, and other modalities in a unified manner. Let's take an example:

Imagine showing a model an image of a dog sitting next to a skateboard and asking, *"What is the dog doing?"* A unimodal text model wouldn't know because it can't see the image. A unimodal vision model might identify a dog and a skateboard but wouldn't infer that the dog is likely sitting idle rather than riding it. A multimodal AI system, however, can **combine the textual prompt with the visual context** to generate a meaningful response, such as, *"The dog is sitting next to the skateboard, possibly waiting for someone to play with it."*

Why Multimodal AI Matters

The ability to process multiple data types together is unlocking new possibilities across industries. **Healthcare, education, entertainment, security, and e-commerce** are just a few areas benefiting from multimodal AI. From **AI-powered tutors that understand both written and spoken queries** to **virtual assistants that can interpret photos and provide recommendations**, the applications are vast.

Multimodal AI also makes AI interactions more natural. Instead of typing out every command, users can speak, show images, or use gestures to communicate with AI systems. This improves accessibility, particularly for those with disabilities, and creates a more seamless user experience.

Looking Ahead

As multimodal AI continues to evolve, we're moving closer to AI systems that **understand and interact with the world more like humans do**. The challenge isn't just about training larger models but about improving efficiency, reducing bias, and ensuring that AI can adapt to real-world scenarios with minimal supervision.

DeepSeek-VL represents a step forward in this field, making **advanced vision-language capabilities accessible to developers and researchers**. In the next sections, we'll explore how DeepSeek-VL works, its architecture, and how you can start using it for real-world applications.

The journey into multimodal AI is just beginning, and it's an exciting time to be a part of it. Let's dive in!

1.2 The Evolution of Vision-Language Models

Artificial Intelligence has come a long way in enabling machines to process language and images. While early AI systems could either recognize images or understand text, they lacked the ability to connect the two seamlessly. The journey toward **vision-language models (VLMs)** has been marked by breakthroughs in deep learning, data availability, and computational power, leading us to powerful systems like **DeepSeek-VL** that can analyze images and text together.

To understand where we are today, it's helpful to look back at how these models evolved—from simple image-captioning systems to sophisticated, multimodal AI that can generate text from images, answer visual questions, and even create entirely new content.

Early Days: Isolated Vision and Language Models

In the early days of AI, **computer vision and natural language processing (NLP) developed separately**. Vision models focused on object detection, classification, and segmentation, while NLP models dealt with tasks like machine translation and text generation. These two fields had little overlap, as AI systems were trained on distinct datasets tailored to their respective domains.

One of the first attempts to bring images and text together was **image captioning**, where a model would generate a description of an image. Early methods used rule-based systems or simple statistical models to generate text based on visual input. However, these models were highly constrained—they could describe only specific objects and struggled with complex scenes or abstract concepts.

Deep Learning and the Rise of Multimodal Models

The real breakthrough came with **deep learning** in the 2010s. Convolutional Neural Networks (CNNs) revolutionized computer vision, allowing AI to identify objects in images with high accuracy. Meanwhile, the development of **word embeddings** like Word2Vec and GloVe improved NLP by capturing the relationships between words.

It wasn't long before researchers started combining these advancements. The **first wave of vision-language models** used CNNs for image feature extraction and recurrent neural networks (RNNs) for text generation. This led to models like **Show and Tell (2015)** by Google, which could generate image captions by combining a CNN with an LSTM (Long Short-Term Memory) network. These models demonstrated that AI could connect images and text, but they still lacked deeper reasoning and struggled with ambiguous images.

Transformers and the Multimodal Revolution

The next major leap came with the introduction of **transformers**, particularly the **Transformer architecture** introduced by Vaswani et al. in 2017. Transformers revolutionized NLP by enabling models like BERT and GPT, which could understand and generate human-like text with remarkable fluency.

Researchers soon realized that transformers could also be applied to multimodal tasks. Instead of treating images and text as separate entities, **new architectures emerged that could process both within a shared model.** Vision-language models like **VL-BERT, UNITER, and LXMERT** integrated transformers to align textual and visual representations.

A significant milestone was **CLIP (Contrastive Language-Image Pretraining)** by OpenAI in 2021. CLIP demonstrated that AI could **learn from massive datasets of image-text pairs** scraped from the internet, enabling it to recognize concepts in images without task-specific training. Instead of being trained on labeled datasets, CLIP learned by associating images with their corresponding textual descriptions. This made it highly generalizable, allowing it to perform zero-shot learning—making accurate predictions on tasks it had never seen before.

The Rise of Large-Scale Vision-Language Models

Following CLIP, the race to build larger and more capable **vision-language models** accelerated. OpenAI's **DALL·E** demonstrated AI's ability to generate images from textual descriptions, showing that multimodal AI could work in reverse—not just understanding images but creating them.

At the same time, models like **Flamingo (by DeepMind), BLIP, and GIT (Generalist Image-to-Text models)** pushed the boundaries further by improving reasoning and contextual understanding. These models were trained on enormous datasets containing millions of image-text pairs, allowing them to perform **visual question answering, image captioning, and even reasoning about complex visual scenes.**

DeepSeek-VL: A New Generation of Vision-Language Models

Now, we are entering an era where vision-language models are not just passive tools but **interactive AI systems** that can reason, generate, and assist in real-world applications. DeepSeek-VL represents the latest step in this journey, bringing **powerful multimodal capabilities to developers**.

DeepSeek-VL builds on previous advancements but focuses on efficiency, accessibility, and real-world usability. Unlike early models that required massive computational resources, DeepSeek-VL is designed to be **developer-friendly**, making it easier to integrate into applications like **chatbots, AI-powered search, medical imaging analysis, and creative content generation.**

Looking Ahead

The future of vision-language models is promising. As AI continues to evolve, we can expect even **better reasoning, more accurate multimodal understanding, and seamless human-AI interaction**. With **improvements in training efficiency and model architectures, VLMs will become more accessible, allowing developers to build powerful AI applications with minimal barriers.**

DeepSeek-VL is a testament to how far we've come, and in the coming chapters, we'll explore how you can leverage it to build cutting-edge multimodal AI applications. Let's dive into the practical aspects of working with DeepSeek-VL and bring multimodal AI to life.

1.3 Why DeepSeek-VL? Key Features and Advantages

Artificial intelligence is advancing rapidly, and vision-language models (VLMs) are at the forefront of this transformation. While many models claim to offer state-of-the-art performance, **DeepSeek-VL stands out due to its efficiency, versatility, and accessibility for developers.** But what exactly makes it unique, and why should you consider using it?

In this section, we'll explore the core strengths of DeepSeek-VL and what sets it apart from other VLMs.

A New Standard in Vision-Language AI

DeepSeek-VL isn't just another multimodal AI model—it's a **next-generation vision-language system** designed to bridge the gap between image and text understanding in a more intuitive and developer-friendly way. Whether you're building chatbots, AI-driven search engines, or creative tools, DeepSeek-VL provides the power to process, interpret, and generate multimodal content with high accuracy.

Unlike earlier VLMs that were either **too resource-intensive** or **too limited in scope**, DeepSeek-VL strikes a balance between **efficiency, accuracy, and usability**, making it one of the most accessible models for developers looking to integrate multimodal AI into real-world applications.

Key Features of DeepSeek-VL

1. Advanced Multimodal Understanding

DeepSeek-VL can analyze images and text simultaneously, allowing for **context-aware responses**. It doesn't just recognize objects in an image; it **understands the relationships between them, interprets textual cues, and generates meaningful insights.**

For example, if given an image of a **crowded marketplace** and asked, *"What is happening here?"* DeepSeek-VL doesn't just list objects (people, stalls, goods); it can **describe the atmosphere, detect interactions between people, and even infer cultural elements based on the scene.**

2. Efficient and Scalable

One of the biggest challenges with VLMs has been their **high computational costs**. Many models require enormous resources, making them impractical for developers without enterprise-level infrastructure. DeepSeek-VL, however, has been optimized for efficiency, ensuring that it can run effectively on **moderate hardware** while still delivering state-of-the-art performance.

This makes it an excellent choice for **startups, research labs, and independent developers** who want powerful vision-language capabilities without excessive computational expenses.

3. Strong Performance on Vision-Language Tasks

DeepSeek-VL has been trained on a vast dataset of **image-text pairs**, allowing it to excel in tasks such as:

- **Image Captioning** – Generating descriptive captions for images with contextual awareness.
- **Visual Question Answering (VQA)** – Answering complex questions about images with high accuracy.
- **Image-Based Reasoning** – Inferring relationships and making logical deductions from visual data.

This level of capability is crucial for applications in **medical imaging, e-commerce, digital content creation, and AI-powered search.**

4. Seamless Integration with AI Workflows

Many VLMs require extensive **fine-tuning and preprocessing** before they can be useful in real applications. DeepSeek-VL, on the other hand, is built with **developer-friendliness in mind**. It offers:

- **Pre-trained models that work out-of-the-box**
- **Easy integration with Python frameworks and APIs**
- **Support for real-time applications**

This makes it easier for businesses and developers to deploy DeepSeek-VL in a variety of **production environments** without months of research and experimentation.

5. Robust Few-Shot and Zero-Shot Learning

Unlike traditional AI models that require large amounts of labeled data, DeepSeek-VL leverages **few-shot and zero-shot learning**, meaning it can:

- **Understand new concepts with minimal examples**
- **Generalize well across different domains**
- **Adapt to new tasks without extensive retraining**

This is particularly useful for **dynamic industries** where AI must keep up with new information—such as news analysis, medical diagnostics, or trend-based content generation.

Advantages of Using DeepSeek-VL

1. Reduces Development Time

Because DeepSeek-VL comes pre-trained on a diverse dataset, it significantly cuts down the time needed to develop **vision-language applications**. Instead of spending weeks gathering training data and fine-tuning a model, developers can quickly plug DeepSeek-VL into their applications and start seeing results.

2. Enhances User Experience in AI Applications

Whether you're building an AI-powered **virtual assistant, search engine, or creative tool**, DeepSeek-VL enhances the user experience by:

- **Understanding images and text together**
- **Generating more natural responses**
- **Improving accuracy in complex queries**

This leads to **more intuitive and interactive AI-driven applications**, boosting engagement and usability.

3. Democratizes Access to Multimodal AI

Many cutting-edge AI models remain **locked behind expensive APIs or proprietary systems**. DeepSeek-VL is designed to be more **accessible**, allowing researchers, small businesses, and independent developers to experiment with and deploy state-of-the-art **vision-language capabilities** without prohibitive costs.

4. Future-Proof AI for Emerging Applications

As AI continues to evolve, **multimodal understanding** will become a critical component of many future applications. DeepSeek-VL is positioned as a **scalable and adaptable solution**, ensuring that developers can **keep up with emerging AI trends** without having to rebuild their entire AI stack.

Why DeepSeek-VL? A Look at the Big Picture

When considering a vision-language model, the key factors to look at are **accuracy, efficiency, adaptability, and ease of use**. DeepSeek-VL excels in all these areas, making it a **practical choice for developers, researchers, and businesses alike**.

Its ability to **process both images and text with high precision, work efficiently on standard hardware, and integrate seamlessly with existing AI pipelines** makes it an outstanding tool for building the next generation of **AI-powered applications.**

In the coming chapters, we'll explore **how to set up DeepSeek-VL, integrate it into different workflows, and use it for real-world tasks.** Whether you're a developer looking to build intelligent applications or a researcher exploring multimodal AI, DeepSeek-VL provides the tools you need to unlock new possibilities.

1.4 Real-World Applications of DeepSeek-VL

Artificial intelligence is reshaping industries at an unprecedented pace, and vision-language models (VLMs) like DeepSeek-VL are playing a critical role in this transformation. These models go beyond traditional AI by enabling machines to **see, read, and understand the world in a way that closely resembles human perception**. But how does this capability translate into real-world applications?

DeepSeek-VL is not just a theoretical advancement; it has **practical, tangible uses** across diverse industries. From automating content creation to enhancing accessibility and improving decision-making in high-stakes fields, its multimodal intelligence is opening up new possibilities.

AI-Powered Search and Recommendation Systems

Search engines and recommendation platforms are moving beyond simple text-based queries. Users increasingly expect search results that integrate **both text and visual content**. DeepSeek-VL enhances this experience by enabling **image-based search, contextual recommendations, and more intuitive interactions**.

For instance, in **e-commerce**, a customer might upload a photo of a product they like and ask, *"Where can I buy something similar?"* Traditional search algorithms would struggle with this query, but DeepSeek-VL can analyze the image, extract relevant attributes, and provide a list of similar products—improving both **search accuracy and user experience**.

Beyond e-commerce, media platforms can leverage DeepSeek-VL for **content discovery**. A streaming service, for example, could analyze a screenshot from a movie and suggest films with **similar aesthetics, themes, or even moods**, making recommendations far more personalized than conventional methods.

Visual Question Answering and Knowledge Extraction

One of the most powerful applications of DeepSeek-VL is **visual question answering (VQA)**—where AI can analyze an image and provide intelligent responses to user queries. This has significant implications for industries where **interpreting visual data is crucial**.

In **education**, students can take a picture of a math problem, a historical artifact, or a complex diagram and ask questions like *"What does this symbol mean?"* or *"Explain this equation step by step."* DeepSeek-VL can provide **detailed explanations, historical context, or even suggest related topics for deeper learning**.

Similarly, in **news and fact-checking**, journalists can use DeepSeek-VL to **extract information from images**, verify authenticity, and cross-reference visual content with textual sources. This is particularly valuable in combating **misinformation and deepfakes**, where AI-driven verification can distinguish between genuine and manipulated media.

Automated Content Generation and Enhancement

Content creation has always been **time-consuming and resource-intensive**, but multimodal AI is streamlining the process. DeepSeek-VL can generate

rich, context-aware captions, articles, and summaries based on images and text, making it an invaluable tool for **journalists, marketers, and creatives**.

Consider an **online publishing platform** that wants to automatically generate descriptions for images in articles. Instead of relying on human writers for every caption, DeepSeek-VL can analyze images and generate **concise, meaningful descriptions** that match the tone and context of the article.

For **social media and digital marketing**, this capability means businesses can create engaging, automated content tailored to specific audiences. An AI-powered system could, for example, generate **Instagram post captions, ad descriptions, or even video summaries** based on uploaded images and video frames.

Accessibility and Assistive Technologies

For individuals with **visual impairments**, technology has been a game-changer, and DeepSeek-VL is pushing accessibility even further. Traditional screen readers rely on **text-to-speech**, but multimodal AI enables a richer, more immersive experience.

Imagine a visually impaired person using a **smartphone camera to explore their surroundings**. With DeepSeek-VL, the AI can **describe the scene, identify objects, read text from images, and even interpret facial expressions or gestures**, allowing for **a more interactive and informative experience**.

In **public spaces**, AI-powered kiosks or mobile applications could provide real-time assistance, helping users navigate **airports, train stations, or shopping centers** by interpreting **signage, maps, and environmental cues**.

Medical and Healthcare Applications

In the medical field, vision-language AI is revolutionizing **diagnostics, patient education, and research**. DeepSeek-VL has the potential to assist doctors and medical professionals in interpreting **medical images, patient charts, and radiology reports** with greater precision.

Consider an **oncologist analyzing an MRI scan**. Instead of manually cross-referencing findings with written reports, DeepSeek-VL can instantly generate **contextual insights**, flagging potential abnormalities and correlating findings with **medical literature and past case studies**.

For **patients**, AI-powered medical assistants can **explain diagnostic images in simpler terms**, making healthcare more transparent and understandable. A patient who receives an X-ray or ultrasound image could upload it to a medical AI assistant and ask, *"What does this image indicate?"*—getting an explanation tailored to their level of understanding.

Security, Surveillance, and Law Enforcement

Vision-language AI is also making strides in **security and surveillance**, where it can be used to analyze visual data for **threat detection, forensic analysis, and criminal investigations**.

For example, **airport security systems** could use DeepSeek-VL to scan CCTV footage and detect **suspicious activities in real-time**, flagging potential threats based on visual patterns and behavior analysis.

In law enforcement, AI-powered tools can assist investigators by analyzing **images from crime scenes, identifying key objects, matching visual evidence with textual reports, and even helping reconstruct crime timelines**. This significantly reduces the time needed to process and analyze **large volumes of visual data**, improving the efficiency of investigations.

The Future of Multimodal AI in Everyday Life

As AI continues to advance, multimodal models like DeepSeek-VL will **seamlessly integrate into our daily lives**. We are already seeing early versions of this in **AI assistants, smart home devices, and AR-powered applications**, but the potential is far greater.

Imagine **AI-driven shopping assistants** that can scan your fridge and suggest recipes based on available ingredients, or **personalized fitness coaches** that analyze exercise videos and provide real-time feedback on form and posture.

Even in **entertainment and gaming**, vision-language AI is opening doors to more interactive storytelling, where AI characters can respond dynamically to both text and visual inputs—blurring the lines between human and AI-driven creativity.

Final Thoughts

DeepSeek-VL is not just a tool—it's a **paradigm shift in how AI interacts with the world**. Its ability to process and understand both images and text is transforming **search, education, healthcare, security, accessibility, and more**. Whether you're a developer, researcher, or entrepreneur, the opportunities to innovate with multimodal AI are endless.

In the next chapters, we'll explore how to **set up DeepSeek-VL, integrate it into workflows, and build real-world applications**. The future of AI is multimodal, and DeepSeek-VL is at the forefront of this revolution. Let's dive deeper into how you can leverage it to build the next generation of intelligent systems.

Chapter 2: Understanding DeepSeek-VL's Architecture

DeepSeek-VL isn't just another AI model—it's a carefully designed system that processes and understands **both images and text** in a unified way. This ability to merge vision and language is what makes it such a powerful tool for applications like **image captioning, visual question answering, and multimodal search**.

To fully leverage DeepSeek-VL, it's important to understand how it works under the hood. In this chapter, we'll break down its architecture, explore how it processes multimodal inputs, and look at the key components that power its performance.

2.1 How Vision-Language Models Process Text and Images

When humans interpret the world around them, we rarely rely on just one sense. Imagine you're at a restaurant, looking at a menu while also seeing dishes being served to other tables. You don't just read the menu—you also **match what you read to the visual cues around you**. Vision-language models (VLMs) attempt to replicate this **multimodal understanding** by processing text and images together.

DeepSeek-VL is one such model that bridges the gap between language and vision, enabling AI to understand and generate responses that integrate both types of information. But how does it actually process these inputs? Let's break it down in a way that's both clear and practical.

From Pixels and Words to Meaning: The Processing Pipeline

At a high level, DeepSeek-VL follows three core steps when working with text and images:

1. **Extracting features from images** – Converting raw pixel data into meaningful numerical representations.

2. **Embedding text** – Transforming words into vectorized representations that can be compared with image features.
3. **Aligning and processing both inputs** – Using a multimodal transformer to find relationships between text and images before generating a response.

Step 1: Extracting Features from Images

When you feed an image into DeepSeek-VL, it doesn't "see" the picture the way humans do. Instead, it analyzes patterns, textures, and objects, converting them into structured data. This is done using an **image encoder**, typically based on a **Vision Transformer (ViT)** or a **Convolutional Neural Network (CNN)**.

The encoder breaks the image into smaller patches (like dividing an image into a grid) and transforms each patch into a **vector representation** that captures its essential features. This step allows the model to recognize objects, their positions, and their relationships.

Hands-On Example: Extracting Image Features

Let's see this process in action using OpenAI's CLIP model, which works similarly to DeepSeek-VL's image encoding process.

```python
----
import torch
import clip
from PIL import Image

# Load CLIP model and preprocessing function
device = "cuda" if torch.cuda.is_available() else "cpu"
model, preprocess = clip.load("ViT-B/32", device=device)

# Load an image and preprocess it
image_path = "sample_image.jpg"  # Use an actual image path
image =
preprocess(Image.open(image_path)).unsqueeze(0).to(device)

# Extract image features
with torch.no_grad():
    image_features = model.encode_image(image)

# Print feature vector shape
print(image_features.shape)  # Output: (1, 512) or similar
```

This code takes an image, processes it through a Vision Transformer, and extracts its **feature vector**—a numerical representation that the model can use for further processing.

Step 2: Embedding Text into a Vector Space

Just like images are converted into feature vectors, text must also be transformed into a numerical format that can be processed alongside image features. This is done using a **text encoder**, which typically relies on a transformer-based model like **BERT, GPT, or a custom language model**.

In DeepSeek-VL, the text is **tokenized** (split into smaller units) and embedded into a **vector space** where similar words have similar numerical representations. This ensures that the AI understands the meaning behind the text rather than just treating it as a sequence of characters.

Hands-On Example: Extracting Text Features

We can modify our previous example to also encode text and compare it with image features.

```python
# Encode a sample text prompt
text = clip.tokenize(["A cat sitting on a
windowsill"]).to(device)

# Extract text features
with torch.no_grad():
    text_features = model.encode_text(text)

# Print feature vector shape
print(text_features.shape)  # Output: (1, 512) or similar
```

Now, we have two different types of data—**an image feature vector and a text feature vector**—that need to be aligned.

Step 3: Aligning and Processing Both Inputs

Once both the image and text are converted into vector representations, they need to be **aligned** within the same space. DeepSeek-VL uses a **multimodal transformer**, which enables the model to:

- **Compare text and images** to determine their relevance to each other.
- **Generate captions or descriptions** based on what's in an image.
- **Answer questions about an image**, integrating contextual understanding from the text.

In models like CLIP, this alignment happens using **contrastive learning**, where the model learns which text-image pairs are correct and which are mismatched. In DeepSeek-VL, this process is extended using more sophisticated **attention mechanisms** that help the model refine its understanding of how images and text interact.

Hands-On Example: Finding the Best Image-Text Match

Let's take our extracted features and see how well they align.

```python
----
import torch.nn.functional as F

# Compute similarity between image and text
similarity = F.cosine_similarity(image_features,
text_features)

# Print similarity score
print(f"Similarity score: {similarity.item():.4f}")
```

A higher similarity score means the text and image are closely related, while a lower score suggests a weaker connection.

Bringing It All Together

The real power of vision-language models like DeepSeek-VL lies in their ability to **seamlessly integrate image and text information**. By encoding both modalities into numerical representations and aligning them within the same space, these models enable **a wide range of applications**, including:

- **Generating accurate image captions**
- **Answering questions about images**
- **Matching product images to search queries**
- **Enhancing accessibility through automated descriptions**

As we move forward in this book, we'll explore how you can use DeepSeek-VL to build real-world applications, from AI-powered search engines to intelligent assistants.

In the next section, we'll take a closer look at the **core architecture** that makes DeepSeek-VL so powerful, including how transformers, encoders, and decoders work together to process multimodal data.

2.2 Key Components: Transformers, Encoders, and Decoders

DeepSeek-VL, like most vision-language models, is built on a powerful architecture that allows it to process both images and text efficiently. At its core, it relies on **transformers, encoders, and decoders**, which work together to extract meaning, align different modalities, and generate responses.

If you've worked with transformers before, you probably know them as the backbone of models like **GPT, BERT, and T5** in NLP. But how do they handle images? And how do they bridge the gap between vision and language? Let's break it down in a practical, easy-to-understand way.

Transformers: The Brains Behind DeepSeek-VL

The transformer architecture is what allows DeepSeek-VL to process and integrate information from multiple modalities. Originally introduced in the famous paper *"Attention Is All You Need"*, transformers have become the gold standard for deep learning models.

Instead of processing data sequentially (like older RNNs), transformers **analyze all input elements in parallel,** using a mechanism called **self-attention** to weigh the importance of each element relative to others. This is crucial for vision-language tasks because it allows the model to relate words to specific parts of an image efficiently.

In DeepSeek-VL, transformers are used in both the **image encoder** and the **language encoder**, and they also power the final **decoder** responsible for generating responses.

Encoders: Extracting Meaning from Images and Text

Encoders play a critical role in **transforming raw data into structured numerical representations**. DeepSeek-VL has two main types of encoders:

- **A vision encoder** that processes images
- **A language encoder** that processes text

Vision Encoder: Turning Images into Feature Vectors

When an image is fed into DeepSeek-VL, it first goes through an encoder, typically based on a **Vision Transformer (ViT)**. The process works as follows:

1. The image is **split into small patches** (like a grid).
2. Each patch is converted into a **vector representation**.
3. The transformer model processes these vectors, learning how different parts of the image relate to each other.

Let's see this in action with a simple implementation using **Hugging Face's** `transformers` **library**.

```python
from transformers import ViTFeatureExtractor, ViTModel
from PIL import Image
import torch

# Load a Vision Transformer model
feature_extractor =
ViTFeatureExtractor.from_pretrained("google/vit-base-patch16-
224-in21k")
model = ViTModel.from_pretrained("google/vit-base-patch16-
224-in21k")

# Load and preprocess an image
image = Image.open("sample_image.jpg")  # Replace with an
actual image
inputs = feature_extractor(images=image, return_tensors="pt")
```

```
# Extract image features
with torch.no_grad():
    outputs = model(**inputs)

# Get the final image representation
image_features = outputs.last_hidden_state[:, 0, :]
print(image_features.shape)  # Output: (1, 768)
```

This code takes an image, passes it through a Vision Transformer, and outputs a **768-dimensional feature vector**, which can be used to understand the image's contents.

Language Encoder: Turning Text into Feature Vectors

The language encoder works similarly but processes text instead of images. It uses a **pretrained transformer-based language model** (like BERT or GPT) to convert words into numerical embeddings.

Here's how we can extract text features using OpenAI's **CLIP model**, which aligns text and images in a shared space:

```python
import clip

# Load CLIP model
device = "cuda" if torch.cuda.is_available() else "cpu"
model, _ = clip.load("ViT-B/32", device=device)

# Encode a text prompt
text = clip.tokenize(["A cat sitting on a
windowsill"]).to(device)

# Extract text features
with torch.no_grad():
    text_features = model.encode_text(text)

print(text_features.shape)  # Output: (1, 512)
```

Now we have **text embeddings** that can be compared with image embeddings, allowing DeepSeek-VL to match text descriptions with relevant images.

Decoders: Generating Intelligent Responses

Once the image and text inputs are encoded, DeepSeek-VL needs to **decode** the information to generate meaningful responses. The decoder is responsible for:

- Generating **image captions**
- Answering **questions about images**
- Producing **detailed descriptions**

The decoder is usually a **causal transformer model** similar to GPT, which predicts the next word in a sequence based on previous inputs.

Hands-On Example: Generating a Caption for an Image

To see how a decoder works, let's use the **BLIP model**, which is designed for **image captioning and vision-language tasks**.

```python
----
from transformers import BlipProcessor,
BlipForConditionalGeneration

# Load BLIP model and processor
processor = BlipProcessor.from_pretrained("Salesforce/blip-
image-captioning-base")
model =
BlipForConditionalGeneration.from_pretrained("Salesforce/blip
-image-captioning-base")

# Load and preprocess an image
image = Image.open("sample_image.jpg")  # Replace with an
actual image
inputs = processor(images=image, return_tensors="pt")

# Generate a caption
with torch.no_grad():
    output = model.generate(**inputs)

# Decode and print the caption
caption = processor.batch_decode(output,
skip_special_tokens=True)[0]
print("Generated Caption:", caption)
```

This implementation loads an image, processes it through the BLIP model, and generates a natural-language description—just like DeepSeek-VL does when answering user queries.

How These Components Work Together

To summarize, DeepSeek-VL processes vision and language inputs in three steps:

1. **The encoder extracts features** from images (using a Vision Transformer) and text (using a Language Transformer).
2. **A multimodal transformer aligns the two representations** in a shared embedding space, learning how text and images relate.
3. **The decoder generates a meaningful output**, whether it's a caption, an answer, or another relevant response.

The combination of transformers, encoders, and decoders allows DeepSeek-VL to **interpret, align, and generate human-like responses** that integrate both vision and language.

In the next section, we'll explore **training data and pretraining techniques**, where we'll see how DeepSeek-VL learns from vast datasets to improve its multimodal understanding.

2.3 Training Data and Pretraining Approaches

Training a vision-language model like DeepSeek-VL is a massive undertaking. It requires large-scale, diverse datasets that combine images and text in meaningful ways, allowing the model to learn how to associate visual elements with language. But data alone isn't enough—how the model is pretrained plays a crucial role in its ability to generate accurate and context-aware outputs.

In this chapter, we'll explore what kind of data DeepSeek-VL is trained on, the pretraining strategies it uses, and how developers can fine-tune similar models for their own applications.

Understanding the Training Data

DeepSeek-VL, like other multimodal AI models, learns from **paired image-text datasets**. These datasets help the model build a shared understanding of

what words correspond to which visual elements. The more diverse and well-labeled the dataset, the better the model becomes at recognizing complex relationships between text and images.

Some commonly used datasets in training vision-language models include:

- **COCO (Common Objects in Context)** – A dataset with images and detailed captions.
- **Conceptual Captions** – Web-scraped image-text pairs with more diverse descriptions.
- **LAION-5B** – A massive open dataset used in models like Stable Diffusion and CLIP.

These datasets ensure the model is exposed to a wide variety of real-world scenarios, reducing bias and improving generalization.

Example: Loading a Vision-Language Dataset in Python

To work with image-text datasets, we can use Hugging Face's `datasets` library. Here's how you can load the **COCO captions dataset** for your own experimentation:

```python
from datasets import load_dataset

# Load COCO dataset with image-text pairs
dataset = load_dataset("hf-internal-testing/coco_captions")

# View a sample
sample = dataset["train"][0]
print("Image:", sample["image"])
print("Caption:", sample["caption"])
```

This dataset provides an image and multiple corresponding captions, making it useful for training multimodal models.

Pretraining Strategies for Vision-Language Models

Pretraining a model like DeepSeek-VL involves more than just feeding it images and captions. The model undergoes **structured learning tasks** that help it understand **alignment** (matching images with correct text), **reasoning** (answering questions about images), and **generation** (creating new captions or descriptions).

Contrastive Learning: Matching Text to the Right Image

One of the most effective pretraining methods is **contrastive learning**, used in models like **CLIP**. The goal is simple:

- The model is given a batch of images and captions.
- It learns to match the correct image-caption pairs while distinguishing them from incorrect ones.

Here's how contrastive learning works in a **real training setup**:

```python
----
import clip
import torch

# Load CLIP model
device = "cuda" if torch.cuda.is_available() else "cpu"
model, preprocess = clip.load("ViT-B/32", device=device)

# Example image and text
from PIL import Image
image =
preprocess(Image.open("sample_image.jpg")).unsqueeze(0).to(device)
text = clip.tokenize(["A cat sitting on a windowsill", "A dog playing in the park"]).to(device)

# Compute image and text embeddings
with torch.no_grad():
    image_features = model.encode_image(image)
    text_features = model.encode_text(text)

# Compute similarity scores
similarity = (image_features @ text_features.T).softmax(dim=-1)
print("Similarity scores:", similarity)
```

This method ensures that the model not only **understands individual images and text** but also **learns how to align them correctly**.

Masked Language Modeling (MLM): Learning to Predict Missing Words

Another pretraining strategy, inspired by BERT, is **Masked Language Modeling (MLM)**. The model is given a sentence with missing words and must predict the masked parts.

For example, given the sentence:

"A [MASK] is sitting on the windowsill."

The model should predict:

"A **cat** is sitting on the windowsill."

Here's how MLM works using **Hugging Face's BERT model**:

```python
from transformers import BertTokenizer, BertForMaskedLM
import torch

# Load pre-trained BERT model
tokenizer = BertTokenizer.from_pretrained("bert-base-uncased")
model = BertForMaskedLM.from_pretrained("bert-base-uncased")

# Tokenize sentence with masked word
sentence = "A [MASK] is sitting on the windowsill."
inputs = tokenizer(sentence, return_tensors="pt")

# Predict masked token
with torch.no_grad():
    outputs = model(**inputs)
    predictions = torch.argmax(outputs.logits, dim=-1)

# Decode predicted token
predicted_word = tokenizer.decode(predictions[0])
print("Predicted Word:", predicted_word)
```

For DeepSeek-VL, this approach helps the model **understand context and predict missing words**, improving its ability to generate natural language responses.

Fine-Tuning a Pretrained Model

Once DeepSeek-VL is pretrained on massive datasets, developers can fine-tune it for **specific applications**, such as medical imaging, autonomous driving, or customer support. Fine-tuning involves training the model on **domain-specific data** to improve accuracy in a specialized field.

Example: Fine-Tuning BLIP for Custom Captioning

If you want to fine-tune a vision-language model like BLIP on your own dataset, here's how you can start:

```python
from transformers import BlipProcessor,
BlipForConditionalGeneration, Trainer, TrainingArguments

# Load the model and processor
processor = BlipProcessor.from_pretrained("Salesforce/blip-image-captioning-base")
model =
BlipForConditionalGeneration.from_pretrained("Salesforce/blip-image-captioning-base")

# Define training parameters
training_args = TrainingArguments(
    output_dir="./fine_tuned_blip",
    per_device_train_batch_size=8,
    per_device_eval_batch_size=8,
    num_train_epochs=3,
    logging_dir="./logs"
)

# Create a Trainer instance
trainer = Trainer(
    model=model,
    args=training_args,
    train_dataset=your_custom_dataset,  # Replace with actual dataset
    eval_dataset=your_validation_dataset
)

# Start training
trainer.train()
```

Fine-tuning allows models like DeepSeek-VL to **adapt to new domains**, making them more useful for real-world applications.

Conclusion

DeepSeek-VL's training pipeline is a combination of **large-scale multimodal datasets** and **intelligent pretraining techniques** like **contrastive learning and masked language modeling**. These methods help the model **learn from images and text in a meaningful way**, allowing it to generate highly accurate responses.

By fine-tuning DeepSeek-VL on specialized datasets, developers can build **custom AI assistants, automated image captioning systems, or even domain-specific chatbots** that truly understand both vision and language.

In the next chapter, we'll **dive into practical implementations**, where we'll walk through how to set up DeepSeek-VL and use it for real-world tasks.

Part 2: Getting Started with DeepSeek-VL

Chapter 3: Setting Up Your Development Environment

Before diving into real-world applications with DeepSeek-VL, you need to set up a working development environment. This involves installing the necessary dependencies, understanding the API and SDK, and running your first DeepSeek-VL model. Whether you're a beginner exploring vision-language models for the first time or an experienced developer integrating DeepSeek-VL into an existing AI pipeline, this chapter will guide you step by step.

3.1 Installing DeepSeek-VL and Dependencies

Getting started with DeepSeek-VL requires setting up a proper development environment. The process is straightforward, but a well-structured setup can save you a lot of headaches later. In this section, we'll walk through installing DeepSeek-VL, configuring dependencies, and ensuring your system is ready to handle vision-language tasks efficiently.

If you've worked with large-scale AI models before, you know that dependency management is crucial. Conflicting libraries, outdated CUDA versions, or missing system packages can turn a simple installation into a troubleshooting nightmare. To avoid these issues, we'll take a structured approach.

Setting Up a Virtual Environment

While it's possible to install everything globally, using a virtual environment keeps your dependencies isolated and prevents conflicts with other projects. Let's start by creating one:

```bash
python -m venv deepseek-vl-env
```

Once created, activate it:

- **On Windows:**

```bash
----
deepseek-vl-env\Scripts\activate
```

- **On macOS/Linux:**

```bash
----
source deepseek-vl-env/bin/activate
```

With your environment activated, everything you install from this point forward will stay contained within this project.

Installing Core Dependencies

DeepSeek-VL is built on top of PyTorch and the Hugging Face `transformers` library. You'll need to install these first. If you're using a GPU, ensure you have the correct CUDA version for PyTorch.

To install PyTorch with CUDA support, run:

```bash
----
pip install torch torchvision torchaudio --index-url
https://download.pytorch.org/whl/cu118
```

For CPU-only installations, use:

```bash
----
pip install torch torchvision torchaudio
```

Next, install the essential libraries for vision-language processing:

```bash
----
pip install transformers datasets opencv-python pillow
```

- **Transformers**: Provides pre-trained models and APIs for text and vision-language tasks.
- **Datasets**: Useful for loading and managing large-scale datasets.

- **OpenCV and PIL (Pillow)**: Handle image preprocessing and manipulation.

Installing DeepSeek-VL

DeepSeek-VL is available as a package through Hugging Face's model hub. To install it, simply run:

```bash
pip install deepseek-vl
```

Alternatively, if the package isn't yet available via PyPI, you can clone the repository and install it manually:

```bash
git clone https://github.com/DeepSeek-AI/DeepSeek-VL.git
cd DeepSeek-VL
pip install -r requirements.txt
```

Once installed, verify that everything is working correctly. Open a Python shell and run:

```python
import torch
from transformers import AutoProcessor,
AutoModelForVision2Seq

# Load model
model_name = "DeepSeekAI/deepseek-vl"
model = AutoModelForVision2Seq.from_pretrained(model_name)
processor = AutoProcessor.from_pretrained(model_name)

print("DeepSeek-VL is installed and ready to use!")
```

If you see the confirmation message, you're good to go!

Verifying GPU Compatibility

DeepSeek-VL performs significantly better on a GPU, especially when processing high-resolution images. To check if PyTorch detects your GPU, run:

```python
import torch
print("CUDA Available:", torch.cuda.is_available())
print("GPU Name:", torch.cuda.get_device_name(0) if
torch.cuda.is_available() else "No GPU detected")
```

If this returns CUDA Available: False, ensure your system has:

- **An NVIDIA GPU**
- **The correct version of CUDA installed**
- **Compatible GPU drivers**

To install CUDA and cuDNN, visit NVIDIA's official CUDA Toolkit page.

First Test: Running a Vision-Language Task

Let's make sure everything is working by passing an image to DeepSeek-VL and generating a description.

```python
from transformers import AutoProcessor,
AutoModelForVision2Seq
from PIL import Image
import torch

# Load DeepSeek-VL model and processor
model_name = "DeepSeekAI/deepseek-vl"
model = AutoModelForVision2Seq.from_pretrained(model_name)
processor = AutoProcessor.from_pretrained(model_name)

# Load an image
image = Image.open("sample_image.jpg")

# Process input
inputs = processor(images=image, return_tensors="pt")

# Generate output
```

```
with torch.no_grad():
    output = model.generate(**inputs)

# Decode output
response = processor.batch_decode(output,
skip_special_tokens=True)[0]
print("Generated Description:", response)
```

If everything is installed correctly, you should see a description of the image printed in the terminal.

Troubleshooting Installation Issues

Even with a well-documented installation process, things don't always go smoothly. Here are some common issues and how to fix them:

1. Torch Installation Errors

If `torch` fails to install, check your Python version. DeepSeek-VL requires **Python 3.8 or later**.

Run:

```bash
----
python --version
```

If your version is outdated, upgrade Python before proceeding.

2. CUDA Not Detected

If PyTorch doesn't recognize your GPU, reinstall the correct CUDA version:

```bash
----
pip uninstall torch torchvision torchaudio
pip install torch torchvision torchaudio --index-url
https://download.pytorch.org/whl/cu118
```

3. ModuleNotFoundError: No module named 'deepseek-vl'

This usually means DeepSeek-VL wasn't installed properly. Try reinstalling:

```
bash
----
pip install --upgrade deepseek-vl
```

Or, if using the GitHub repo:

```
bash
----
cd DeepSeek-VL
pip install -e .
```

Next Steps

Now that your development environment is set up and DeepSeek-VL is running, you're ready to dive into **API usage and SDK integration**. In the next section, we'll explore how to interact with the model programmatically, fine-tune inputs, and get the most out of DeepSeek-VL.

3.2 API Usage and SDK Integration

Now that DeepSeek-VL is installed, it's time to interact with it programmatically. The model provides a straightforward API for processing images and generating text descriptions, making it easy to integrate into various applications. Whether you're building an AI-powered assistant, an automated image captioning tool, or an advanced multimodal search engine, knowing how to use the API efficiently is crucial.

In this section, we'll explore how to load the model, process input data, and generate outputs using the DeepSeek-VL API. We'll also cover SDK integration for more advanced use cases, ensuring you have a solid foundation to start building real-world applications.

Loading the DeepSeek-VL Model

DeepSeek-VL is built on Hugging Face's `transformers` library, which makes loading and interacting with the model intuitive. Start by importing the required libraries and initializing the model:

```python
from transformers import AutoProcessor,
AutoModelForVision2Seq
import torch
from PIL import Image
import requests

# Load DeepSeek-VL model and processor
model_name = "DeepSeekAI/deepseek-vl"
model = AutoModelForVision2Seq.from_pretrained(model_name)
processor = AutoProcessor.from_pretrained(model_name)
```

This setup ensures that both the model and processor are loaded into memory. If this is your first time running the code, Hugging Face will download the necessary files automatically.

Processing an Image with the API

To generate meaningful insights from an image, we need to preprocess it and pass it through the model. Let's try with an example image:

```python
# Load an image from a URL
image_url = "https://example.com/sample-image.jpg"  # Replace
with a real URL
image = Image.open(requests.get(image_url, stream=True).raw)

# Preprocess the image
inputs = processor(images=image, return_tensors="pt")

# Generate a response
with torch.no_grad():
    output = model.generate(**inputs)

# Decode the output
response = processor.batch_decode(output,
skip_special_tokens=True)[0]
print("Generated Description:", response)
```

Here, we fetch an image from a URL, process it into the correct format, and generate a textual description. The response will contain a natural-language interpretation of the image.

If you prefer to use a local image instead of fetching from a URL, simply replace the `image_url` section with:

```python
image = Image.open("path/to/your/image.jpg")
```

Integrating DeepSeek-VL into an Application

Using DeepSeek-VL for Automated Captioning

One practical application of DeepSeek-VL is automated image captioning. Let's create a simple script that takes an image as input and returns a detailed caption:

```python
def generate_caption(image_path):
    image = Image.open(image_path)
    inputs = processor(images=image, return_tensors="pt")

    with torch.no_grad():
        output = model.generate(**inputs)

    return processor.batch_decode(output,
skip_special_tokens=True)[0]

# Example usage
caption = generate_caption("sample_image.jpg")
print("Image Caption:", caption)
```

This function can be embedded in a larger application, such as an accessibility tool for visually impaired users or an automated tagging system for image databases.

DeepSeek-VL API Integration with FastAPI

To expose DeepSeek-VL as a REST API, we can use **FastAPI**, a lightweight and high-performance framework for building APIs with Python. This allows external applications to send an image and receive a textual response.

Setting Up the API

First, install FastAPI and Uvicorn if you haven't already:

```bash
pip install fastapi uvicorn
```

Now, create an API script:

```python
from fastapi import FastAPI, UploadFile, File
from transformers import AutoProcessor,
AutoModelForVision2Seq
from PIL import Image
import torch
import io

# Initialize FastAPI app
app = FastAPI()

# Load model and processor
model_name = "DeepSeekAI/deepseek-v1"
model = AutoModelForVision2Seq.from_pretrained(model_name)
processor = AutoProcessor.from_pretrained(model_name)

@app.post("/generate-caption/")
async def generate_caption(file: UploadFile = File(...)):
    image = Image.open(io.BytesIO(await file.read()))
    inputs = processor(images=image, return_tensors="pt")

    with torch.no_grad():
        output = model.generate(**inputs)

    caption = processor.batch_decode(output,
skip_special_tokens=True)[0]
    return {"caption": caption}
```

To run the API, save this script as `app.py` and start the FastAPI server:

```bash
uvicorn app:app --host 0.0.0.0 --port 8000
```

Now, you can send an image via an API request to `http://localhost:8000/generate-caption/`, and it will return a caption for the image.

Extending Functionality with SDKs

DeepSeek-VL can be integrated into applications beyond direct API calls. If the model is integrated into an SDK, you can work with it more efficiently within an existing software ecosystem. Here's an example of how SDK integration might look:

```python
from deepseek_vl_sdk import DeepSeekVL

# Initialize SDK client
client = DeepSeekVL(api_key="your_api_key")

# Process image through SDK
response = client.describe_image("sample_image.jpg")

print("SDK Response:", response)
```

An SDK would typically handle authentication, error management, and optimized performance under the hood. If DeepSeek-VL releases an official SDK, this would be the preferred method for large-scale applications.

Key Takeaways

- DeepSeek-VL's API is built on Hugging Face's `transformers` library, making it easy to use.
- Processing an image requires loading it, transforming it into tensors, and passing it through the model.
- DeepSeek-VL can be integrated into web applications using FastAPI, allowing external services to interact with the model.
- Future SDKs may provide more streamlined integration for enterprise use cases.

In the next section, we'll run **our first DeepSeek-VL model on a real dataset** to see how it performs in practical scenarios.

3.3 Running Your First DeepSeek-VL Model

Now that we have installed DeepSeek-VL and explored its API, it's time to put everything into action. Running the model for the first time is an exciting step because it allows us to see how DeepSeek-VL processes images and generates meaningful outputs.

In this section, we'll guide you through loading the model, running it on sample images, and interpreting the results. By the end, you'll have a fully functional setup capable of generating insights from multimodal inputs.

Loading the Model and Processor

DeepSeek-VL is built using Hugging Face's `transformers` library, so initializing it is straightforward. Let's start by loading the model and processor:

```python
from transformers import AutoProcessor,
AutoModelForVision2Seq
import torch

# Load the model and processor
model_name = "DeepSeekAI/deepseek-vl"
model = AutoModelForVision2Seq.from_pretrained(model_name)
processor = AutoProcessor.from_pretrained(model_name)
```

This step ensures the model is available for use. If this is your first time running the code, Hugging Face will automatically download the necessary files.

Processing an Image Input

Let's test DeepSeek-VL with a sample image. We'll use a simple example where the model generates a caption for an image:

```python
from PIL import Image
import requests

# Load an image from a URL
image_url = "https://example.com/sample-image.jpg"  # Replace
with a real image URL
image = Image.open(requests.get(image_url, stream=True).raw)
```

```
# Preprocess the image for the model
inputs = processor(images=image, return_tensors="pt")

# Generate output
with torch.no_grad():
    output = model.generate(**inputs)

# Decode and print the result
result = processor.batch_decode(output,
skip_special_tokens=True)[0]
print("Generated Output:", result)
```

This script takes an image, processes it using the DeepSeek-VL model, and prints out the generated text. The output could be a caption describing the image or an interpretation of its contents.

For local images, replace the `image_url` section with:

```python
----
image = Image.open("path/to/your/image.jpg")
```

Running a Question-Answering Task

Beyond image captioning, DeepSeek-VL can also handle **vision-language question-answering** (VQA). This means you can ask questions about an image, and the model will generate relevant responses.

Let's try an example where we provide an image and ask a question:

```python
----
# Define a question about the image
question = "What is the person in the image doing?"

# Tokenize the question
inputs = processor(images=image, text=question,
return_tensors="pt")

# Generate an answer
with torch.no_grad():
    output = model.generate(**inputs)

# Decode the response
answer = processor.batch_decode(output,
skip_special_tokens=True)[0]
```

```
print("Model's Answer:", answer)
```

This approach enables interactive applications, such as smart assistants and AI-driven visual analysis tools.

Expanding the Experiment: Batch Processing

What if you need to process multiple images at once? DeepSeek-VL can handle **batch processing**, allowing you to analyze several images in one go.

```python
# Load multiple images
image_paths = ["image1.jpg", "image2.jpg", "image3.jpg"]
images = [Image.open(img_path) for img_path in image_paths]

# Process all images in a batch
inputs = processor(images=images, return_tensors="pt")

# Generate captions
with torch.no_grad():
    outputs = model.generate(**inputs)

# Decode and print results
captions = processor.batch_decode(outputs,
skip_special_tokens=True)
for i, caption in enumerate(captions):
    print(f"Image {i+1}: {caption}")
```

This approach is useful for applications like automated content tagging or visual search engines.

Common Errors and How to Fix Them

When running DeepSeek-VL for the first time, you might encounter a few common issues:

1. **CUDA Out of Memory Error**
   o DeepSeek-VL is a large model and requires a decent GPU. If you run into memory issues, try using a **smaller batch size** or running the model on **CPU mode**:

```python
----
model.to("cpu")
```

2. **Slow Inference Speed**
   - o If inference is too slow, consider using **FP16 precision** (if your GPU supports it):

```python
----
model.half()
```

3. **Incorrect Image Format**
   - o Ensure images are in a format readable by PIL (JPEG, PNG). If an error occurs, convert the image manually:

```python
----
image = image.convert("RGB")
```

Key Takeaways

- DeepSeek-VL can process images to generate descriptions and answer questions about visual content.
- The API allows both **single-image** and **batch processing**, making it useful for various applications.
- When running into errors, adjusting device settings (CPU/GPU) and model precision can help improve performance.

Now that we've successfully run our first DeepSeek-VL model, let's move on to exploring how to fine-tune and customize it for specific use cases in the next chapter!

Chapter 4: Core Capabilities and Use Cases

DeepSeek-VL isn't just another AI model—it's a powerful tool that bridges the gap between visual and textual understanding. At its core, it can generate captions for images, retrieve relevant images based on text queries, and even answer complex questions about visual content. These capabilities make it invaluable in fields like content generation, search engines, accessibility tools, and AI-driven assistants.

In this chapter, we'll explore three key use cases of DeepSeek-VL: **image-to-text (caption generation), text-to-image retrieval, and visual question answering (VQA)**. Each section will break down the concept, provide real-world applications, and walk through practical implementation with code.

4.1 Image-to-Text (Caption Generation)

Imagine scrolling through your photo gallery, and instead of manually adding captions, an AI generates them for you:
"A golden retriever playing in the park on a sunny day."
"A steaming cup of coffee on a wooden table near an open book."

That's the power of **image captioning**—the ability of AI to look at an image and describe it in natural language. DeepSeek-VL brings this capability to life by combining **computer vision** and **natural language processing (NLP)** to create meaningful and contextually accurate captions.

In this section, we'll explore **how DeepSeek-VL generates captions**, its real-world applications, and a hands-on implementation that you can try for yourself.

How Does Image Captioning Work?

At a high level, DeepSeek-VL follows a simple but powerful process:

1. **Image Encoding** – The model analyzes the image using a **vision transformer (ViT)** to extract visual features.
2. **Feature Mapping** – These visual features are then transformed into a structured representation that can be interpreted by the language model.

3. **Text Generation** – A **language model (like a transformer-based decoder)** takes these representations and generates a descriptive caption.

By leveraging a large dataset of **images and their corresponding textual descriptions**, the model learns to **associate visual patterns with natural language expressions**.

Why Is Image Captioning Important?

Image captioning is more than just an AI-powered convenience—it has far-reaching applications:

- **Accessibility** – Screen readers use image captions to describe pictures for visually impaired users.
- **Content Automation** – AI-powered captioning can help automate **social media posts**, news reports, and product listings.
- **Image Search Optimization** – Automatically generated captions improve **search engine discoverability** by providing textual context for images.
- **Digital Asset Management** – Organizing and categorizing large collections of images becomes easier when they have meaningful captions.

Now, let's put DeepSeek-VL to work and generate captions for some images!

Hands-on Implementation: Generating Captions with DeepSeek-VL

To follow along, make sure you have Python installed along with the required libraries. We'll be using **DeepSeek-VL's pretrained model** to generate captions.

Step 1: Install Dependencies

Before running the model, install the necessary packages:

```bash
pip install transformers torch pillow requests
```

The **transformers** library from Hugging Face provides prebuilt models, while **Pillow** handles image processing.

Step 2: Load DeepSeek-VL and Process an Image

Let's load the model and process an image for caption generation.

```python
from transformers import AutoProcessor,
AutoModelForVision2Seq
import torch
from PIL import Image
import requests

# Load the DeepSeek-VL model and processor
model_name = "DeepSeekAI/deepseek-vl"
model = AutoModelForVision2Seq.from_pretrained(model_name)
processor = AutoProcessor.from_pretrained(model_name)

# Load an image from the web
image_url = "https://example.com/sample-image.jpg"  # Replace
with a real image URL
image = Image.open(requests.get(image_url, stream=True).raw)

# Preprocess the image for the model
inputs = processor(images=image, return_tensors="pt")

# Generate a caption
with torch.no_grad():
    output = model.generate(**inputs)

# Decode and print the caption
caption = processor.batch_decode(output,
skip_special_tokens=True)[0]
print("Generated Caption:", caption)
```

Step 3: Understanding the Code

- **AutoProcessor** – Prepares the image for the model.
- **AutoModelForVision2Seq** – Loads the DeepSeek-VL model for **vision-to-text tasks**.
- **generate()** – Runs inference on the image and produces a text caption.

Try replacing the **image URL** with different images to test how well the model generates captions for various scenes.

Enhancing Captions with Fine-Tuning

While the pretrained DeepSeek-VL model is powerful, you can fine-tune it for **specific domains** (e.g., medical imaging, sports photography) to improve accuracy. Fine-tuning involves:

1. **Gathering labeled image-caption pairs**
2. **Training the model on your dataset**
3. **Evaluating and optimizing performance**

Fine-tuning will be covered in **later chapters**, where we explore customizing DeepSeek-VL for specialized applications.

Final Thoughts

Image captioning with DeepSeek-VL is a powerful tool with applications across various industries. Whether you're building **AI-powered social media tools, automated content generators**, or **accessibility solutions**, DeepSeek-VL provides an efficient way to bridge the gap between images and text.

Next, we'll explore another key capability—**text-to-image retrieval**, which allows AI to find relevant images based on textual descriptions.

4.2 Text-to-Image Retrieval

Imagine searching for an image of a **"sunset over the mountains"** in a massive digital library. Instead of manually browsing through thousands of files, an AI-powered system instantly retrieves the most relevant images based on your description.

This is the power of **text-to-image retrieval**, an essential capability in multimodal AI that allows models like DeepSeek-VL to **connect textual descriptions with visual content**.

In this section, we'll explore how **text-to-image retrieval works**, its real-world applications, and provide a hands-on guide to implementing it using DeepSeek-VL.

How Does Text-to-Image Retrieval Work?

At its core, text-to-image retrieval involves three main steps:

1. **Feature Extraction** – The model converts both **text and images into numerical embeddings** using a shared space where they can be compared.
2. **Similarity Matching** – The system finds images whose **visual embeddings closely match the text embeddings** based on cosine similarity or other ranking methods.
3. **Retrieval & Ranking** – The most relevant images are retrieved and ranked by relevance to the text query.

DeepSeek-VL achieves this by leveraging **transformer-based architectures**, particularly **dual encoders**, which process text and images separately but map them to a common representation space.

Why Is Text-to-Image Retrieval Important?

This technology has practical applications across multiple industries:

- **Search Engines** – Platforms like Google Images allow users to find relevant visuals using natural language descriptions.
- **E-Commerce** – Online stores use this to help customers find products by describing them.
- **Media & Journalism** – News organizations can quickly retrieve relevant images for stories without relying on manual tagging.
- **Content Moderation** – AI can flag or retrieve inappropriate images based on textual descriptions.

Now, let's implement a simple **text-to-image retrieval system** using DeepSeek-VL.

Hands-on Implementation: Retrieving Images with DeepSeek-VL

To follow along, ensure you have Python installed along with the required libraries.

Step 1: Install Dependencies

We need Hugging Face's `transformers` library along with `torch` for model execution.

```bash
pip install transformers torch faiss-cpu pillow requests
```

Here, **FAISS (Facebook AI Similarity Search)** helps efficiently search for similar embeddings, which is useful when working with a large collection of images.

Step 2: Load DeepSeek-VL and Prepare Data

We'll use DeepSeek-VL to encode both **text queries and images**, then compare their similarity to retrieve the best-matching image.

```python
from transformers import AutoProcessor, AutoModel
import torch
import faiss
from PIL import Image
import requests

# Load the DeepSeek-VL model and processor
model_name = "DeepSeekAI/deepseek-vl"
model = AutoModel.from_pretrained(model_name)
processor = AutoProcessor.from_pretrained(model_name)

# Function to encode images into embeddings
def encode_image(image_path):
    image = Image.open(image_path).convert("RGB")
    inputs = processor(images=image, return_tensors="pt")
    with torch.no_grad():
        embedding = model.get_image_features(**inputs)
    return embedding.squeeze().numpy()
```

```
# Function to encode text queries into embeddings
def encode_text(text):
    inputs = processor(text=text, return_tensors="pt")
    with torch.no_grad():
        embedding = model.get_text_features(**inputs)
    return embedding.squeeze().numpy()
```

This script defines two functions:

- `encode_image(image_path)`: Converts an image into a numerical embedding.
- `encode_text(text)`: Converts a text query into an embedding.

Step 3: Indexing Images for Retrieval

To perform retrieval, we first need to index a collection of images in an embedding database.

```python
----
# Sample image paths (replace with your dataset)
image_paths = ["image1.jpg", "image2.jpg", "image3.jpg"]

# Encode all images into embeddings
image_embeddings = [encode_image(img) for img in image_paths]

# Convert to FAISS index for fast retrieval
image_index = faiss.IndexFlatL2(len(image_embeddings[0]))
image_index.add(torch.tensor(image_embeddings).numpy())
```

This step:

- Loads multiple images
- Converts them into embeddings
- Stores them in a **FAISS index** for efficient searching

Step 4: Performing Text-to-Image Search

Now, let's use a **text query** to find the most relevant image.

```python
----
# Example text query
query_text = "A dog running on the beach"
query_embedding = encode_text(query_text)

# Search the FAISS index
_, closest_match =
image_index.search(query_embedding.reshape(1, -1), k=1)

# Retrieve and display the best-matching image
best_match_image = image_paths[closest_match[0][0]]
print("Best matching image:", best_match_image)
```

This script:

- Converts the text query into an embedding
- Searches the **FAISS index** for the closest match
- Returns the **best-matching image**

Customizing for Real-World Use

If you're working with a **large-scale image database**, consider:

- **Fine-tuning DeepSeek-VL** on a specific dataset (e.g., medical images, product catalogs).
- **Optimizing FAISS** by using advanced indexing techniques like **IVF (Inverted File Index)** for faster searches.
- **Integrating with a web app** for a user-friendly interface.

Final Thoughts

Text-to-image retrieval is a powerful capability that enables **seamless interaction between text and visual data**. Whether you're building an **AI-powered search engine**, an **e-commerce recommendation system**, or a **media retrieval tool**, DeepSeek-VL provides a strong foundation.

In the next section, we'll explore **Visual Question Answering (VQA)**—another exciting application that allows AI to **answer questions based on image content**.

4.3 Visual Question Answering (VQA)

Imagine you're looking at a complex image, like a crowded marketplace, and you ask, **"How many people are wearing red shirts?"** Instead of manually counting, an AI system processes the image and provides an accurate response.

This is the power of **Visual Question Answering (VQA)**—a groundbreaking capability in multimodal AI where models like **DeepSeek-VL** can **analyze an image and answer textual questions about it**.

In this section, we'll explore how VQA works, its applications, and implement a hands-on example using DeepSeek-VL.

How Does Visual Question Answering Work?

VQA systems follow a structured process:

1. **Understanding the Question** – The model processes the input text to grasp its intent (e.g., counting, identifying, or describing objects).
2. **Analyzing the Image** – The visual input is processed using a transformer-based vision model to extract relevant features.
3. **Multimodal Fusion** – The text and image embeddings are combined in a shared space to determine the best possible answer.
4. **Generating the Answer** – The model predicts the answer based on learned knowledge and context.

DeepSeek-VL is designed to **efficiently handle complex visual queries**, making it a robust choice for VQA applications.

Why Is VQA Important?

VQA has transformed how AI interacts with visual content. It is widely used in:

- **Assistive Technology** – Helping visually impaired users understand images through textual descriptions.

- **E-Commerce** – Allowing shoppers to ask detailed questions about products based on images.
- **Education & Research** – Assisting students in learning by answering questions about historical or scientific images.
- **Medical Diagnostics** – Helping doctors analyze medical scans by answering queries related to anomalies or structures.

Now, let's implement a **VQA system using DeepSeek-VL**.

Hands-on Implementation: Building a VQA System with DeepSeek-VL

Before running the code, ensure you have installed the required dependencies.

Step 1: Install Required Libraries

```bash
pip install transformers torch pillow requests
```

This installs **Hugging Face's transformers** (to load DeepSeek-VL), **Torch** (for model execution), and **Pillow** (to handle image processing).

Step 2: Load DeepSeek-VL and Process Inputs

Now, let's set up our **VQA model** and prepare an image and question for analysis.

```python
from transformers import AutoProcessor,
AutoModelForVision2Seq
import torch
from PIL import Image
import requests

# Load the DeepSeek-VL model and processor
model_name = "DeepSeekAI/deepseek-vl"
processor = AutoProcessor.from_pretrained(model_name)
model = AutoModelForVision2Seq.from_pretrained(model_name)
```

```python
# Function to answer questions based on an image
def answer_question(image_path, question):
    image = Image.open(image_path).convert("RGB")

    # Preprocess inputs
    inputs = processor(images=image, text=question,
return_tensors="pt")

    # Generate answer
    with torch.no_grad():
        output = model.generate(**inputs)

    # Decode and return the response
    answer = processor.decode(output[0],
skip_special_tokens=True)
    return answer
```

Here's what the function does:

- **Loads the image and question**
- **Processes them into model-compatible inputs**
- **Generates a response using DeepSeek-VL**
- **Decodes and returns the predicted answer**

Step 3: Running the VQA Model

Let's test our system using a sample image and question.

```python
# Sample image URL
image_url = "https://example.com/sample_image.jpg"  # Replace
with a real image URL
image_path = "sample.jpg"

# Download and save the image
image = Image.open(requests.get(image_url, stream=True).raw)
image.save(image_path)

# Ask a question about the image
question = "What is the person in the image holding?"
answer = answer_question(image_path, question)

print("Question:", question)
print("Answer:", answer)
```

This code:

- **Downloads an image from a URL**
- **Processes it with a text question**
- **Retrieves the AI-generated response**

Enhancing the VQA System

If you're working with **large datasets or real-time applications**, consider:

- **Fine-tuning DeepSeek-VL** on domain-specific images (e.g., medical, industrial, fashion).
- **Integrating with a chatbot** to enable conversational image-based Q&A.
- **Optimizing response accuracy** by refining the **preprocessing and text prompts**.

Final Thoughts

VQA represents a major leap in **multimodal AI**, allowing systems to **understand and reason about images in human-like ways**. Whether you're building an **interactive assistant**, an **AI tutor**, or a **smart search engine**, DeepSeek-VL makes it possible to deploy **powerful visual question-answering models** with ease.

In the next chapter, we'll explore how to **fine-tune DeepSeek-VL for domain-specific applications** to further enhance its performance.

Part 3: Building and Customizing DeepSeek-VL Models

Chapter 5: Fine-Tuning DeepSeek-VL for Custom Applications

DeepSeek-VL is a powerful out-of-the-box vision-language model, but its true potential is unlocked when fine-tuned on domain-specific data. Whether you're working in **healthcare, e-commerce, robotics, or education**, adapting DeepSeek-VL to specialized tasks can significantly improve accuracy and relevance.

In this chapter, we'll walk through the process of fine-tuning DeepSeek-VL, from **preparing datasets** to **applying transfer learning strategies** and **evaluating model performance**.

5.1 Preparing Datasets for Fine-Tuning

Fine-tuning DeepSeek-VL requires **high-quality datasets** that align with your specific application. Whether you're building a **medical assistant, an e-commerce recommendation system, or an automated captioning tool**, the dataset you choose plays a critical role in model performance.

In this section, we'll go step by step through **selecting, formatting, and preprocessing** datasets for fine-tuning DeepSeek-VL. By the end, you'll have a structured dataset ready for training.

Choosing the Right Dataset

The dataset should be **diverse, balanced, and well-annotated**. Depending on your task, you might use an **existing dataset** or create a **custom one**.

If you're working on **image captioning**, datasets like **COCO Captions** or **Conceptual Captions** offer rich image-text pairs. For **Visual Question Answering (VQA)**, options like **VQA v2** and **GQA** provide diverse question-answer pairs. If you're focused on **text-to-image retrieval**, datasets like **MS MARCO Image Retrieval** can help.

For domain-specific applications like **healthcare or finance**, it's often necessary to build a **custom dataset** tailored to your needs.

Structuring Your Dataset

A **well-structured dataset** ensures that DeepSeek-VL learns effectively. Typically, datasets contain images with corresponding **text descriptions, questions, or search queries**.

Here's an example of a dataset format for **image-to-text captioning**:

```json
[
  {
    "image": "images/cat.jpg",
    "caption": "A fluffy orange cat sitting on a wooden table."
  },
  {
    "image": "images/dog.jpg",
    "caption": "A black and white dog playing with a red ball in the park."
  }
]
```

For **VQA tasks**, the dataset might look like this:

```json
[
  {
    "image": "images/basketball.jpg",
    "question": "What sport is being played?",
    "answer": "Basketball"
  },
  {
    "image": "images/restaurant.jpg",
    "question": "How many people are sitting at the table?",
    "answer": "Four"
  }
]
```

And for **text-to-image retrieval**, the dataset should map multiple descriptions to an image:

json

[
  {
    "image": "images/sunset.jpg",
    "captions": [
      "A beautiful sunset over the ocean.",
      "The sun setting with orange and pink hues in the sky."
    ]
  }
]

Preprocessing Data for DeepSeek-VL

Before using the dataset, **image preprocessing and text normalization** are essential.

1. Loading and Resizing Images

DeepSeek-VL expects **consistent image dimensions**. We can use `PIL` and `torchvision` to preprocess images.

```python
from PIL import Image
import torchvision.transforms as transforms

# Define image transformations
transform = transforms.Compose([
    transforms.Resize((224, 224)),   # Resize to model's
expected input size
    transforms.ToTensor(),            # Convert image to tensor
    transforms.Normalize(mean=[0.5, 0.5, 0.5], std=[0.5, 0.5,
0.5])   # Normalize
])

# Load and preprocess an image
def preprocess_image(image_path):
    image = Image.open(image_path).convert("RGB")
    return transform(image)

# Example usage
image_tensor = preprocess_image("images/cat.jpg")
print("Processed image shape:", image_tensor.shape)
```

This ensures that images are **uniform in size and normalized**, improving model consistency.

2. Cleaning and Tokenizing Text Data

Text annotations need **cleaning and tokenization** before training. Common steps include **lowercasing, removing special characters, and tokenizing text into subwords**.

```python
import re
from transformers import AutoTokenizer

# Load DeepSeek-VL tokenizer
tokenizer = AutoTokenizer.from_pretrained("DeepSeekAI/deepseek-vl")

# Function to clean and tokenize text
def preprocess_text(text):
    text = text.lower()  # Convert to lowercase
    text = re.sub(r"[^a-zA-Z0-9?.!,']", " ", text)  # Remove special characters
    return tokenizer(text, padding="max_length", truncation=True, return_tensors="pt")

# Example usage
sample_text = "A fluffy orange cat sitting on a wooden table."
tokenized_text = preprocess_text(sample_text)
print("Tokenized output:", tokenized_text["input_ids"])
```

Tokenizing text this way ensures it aligns with the model's input requirements.

Combining Images and Text into a Training Dataset

Once the images and text are preprocessed, they need to be **combined into a PyTorch dataset** for fine-tuning.

```python
import torch
from torch.utils.data import Dataset, DataLoader

class VisionLanguageDataset(Dataset):
```

```python
    def __init__(self, data, transform, tokenizer):
        self.data = data
        self.transform = transform
        self.tokenizer = tokenizer

    def __len__(self):
        return len(self.data)

    def __getitem__(self, idx):
        item = self.data[idx]
        image =
self.transform(Image.open(item["image"]).convert("RGB"))
        text = self.tokenizer(item["caption"],
padding="max_length", truncation=True, return_tensors="pt")
        return {"image": image, "text":
text["input_ids"].squeeze(0)}

# Load dataset JSON
import json
with open("dataset.json", "r") as f:
    dataset_json = json.load(f)

# Create dataset instance
dataset = VisionLanguageDataset(dataset_json, transform,
tokenizer)

# Create DataLoader
dataloader = DataLoader(dataset, batch_size=4, shuffle=True)

# Check first batch
for batch in dataloader:
    print("Batch image shape:", batch["image"].shape)
    print("Batch text shape:", batch["text"].shape)
    break
```

This **prepares data efficiently** for training DeepSeek-VL, ensuring images and text are **correctly formatted**.

Final Thoughts

A well-prepared dataset is **key to fine-tuning success**. Whether you're using a **pre-existing dataset or creating a custom one**, the right **formatting, preprocessing, and structuring** will determine how well DeepSeek-VL adapts to your task.

Now that we have a properly structured dataset, the next step is **applying transfer learning techniques** to fine-tune DeepSeek-VL for our specific use case. We'll explore this in the next section.

5.2 Transfer Learning Strategies

Fine-tuning a large-scale vision-language model like DeepSeek-VL from scratch is computationally expensive and requires vast amounts of data. Instead of training from zero, **transfer learning** helps us adapt a pre-trained model to a specific domain or task. This section explores **effective strategies for transfer learning** with DeepSeek-VL and provides practical code implementations to get you started.

Understanding Transfer Learning in DeepSeek-VL

Transfer learning allows us to **leverage knowledge** from a model trained on large-scale datasets and fine-tune it on a smaller, task-specific dataset. This reduces training time, improves performance, and makes deep learning **accessible even with limited resources**.

DeepSeek-VL has been trained on diverse multimodal data, making it capable of **image captioning, visual question answering (VQA), and text-to-image retrieval** out of the box. However, fine-tuning it on **domain-specific datasets** (e.g., medical imaging, e-commerce, or scientific research) can further enhance its accuracy.

Choosing the Right Transfer Learning Approach

The best approach depends on the available **dataset size, computational power, and desired outcome**. Here are the most effective strategies:

1. Feature Extraction (Freezing the Model)

If you have **a small dataset**, it's best to **freeze most of the model's layers** and only train the final layers. This approach retains the general knowledge from the pre-trained DeepSeek-VL model while allowing minor task-specific adjustments.

2. Fine-Tuning (Unfreezing the Model Partially or Fully)

If you have **a larger dataset and computational resources**, fine-tuning **specific layers** or **the entire model** can lead to better performance. This strategy is useful for tasks where pre-trained knowledge is insufficient, such as **medical imaging or domain-specific object recognition**.

3. Adapter Layers (Parameter-Efficient Fine-Tuning - PEFT)

For **low-resource environments**, adding **adapter layers** (LoRA, Prefix Tuning, or BitFit) allows fine-tuning with **fewer trainable parameters**, significantly reducing computational cost.

Hands-On: Fine-Tuning DeepSeek-VL

Let's implement fine-tuning using Hugging Face's `transformers` library.

Step 1: Load Pre-Trained DeepSeek-VL

```python
from transformers import AutoModel, AutoTokenizer

# Load the pre-trained DeepSeek-VL model and tokenizer
model_name = "DeepSeekAI/deepseek-vl"
tokenizer = AutoTokenizer.from_pretrained(model_name)
model = AutoModel.from_pretrained(model_name)

# Print model architecture
print(model)
```

This loads the model with its pre-trained weights. By default, the model is **ready for inference**, meaning we need to **enable training mode** for fine-tuning.

Step 2: Freezing Layers for Feature Extraction

For feature extraction, **we freeze all layers except the final output layers** so that only a few parameters get updated during training.

```python
for param in model.parameters():
    param.requires_grad = False  # Freeze all layers

# Unfreeze the last few layers
for param in model.encoder.layer[-2:].parameters():
    param.requires_grad = True
```

This approach is useful if you **don't have a large dataset** but still need some task-specific adaptation.

Step 3: Preparing the Dataset for Fine-Tuning

We need to **tokenize text inputs and preprocess images** before feeding them into the model. Let's define a dataset class for this.

```python
import torch
from torch.utils.data import Dataset, DataLoader
from PIL import Image
import torchvision.transforms as transforms

class VisionLanguageDataset(Dataset):
    def __init__(self, data, tokenizer, transform):
        self.data = data
        self.tokenizer = tokenizer
        self.transform = transform

    def __len__(self):
        return len(self.data)

    def __getitem__(self, idx):
        item = self.data[idx]
        image = Image.open(item["image"]).convert("RGB")
        image = self.transform(image)

        text = self.tokenizer(item["caption"],
padding="max_length", truncation=True, return_tensors="pt")
```

```
        return {"image": image, "text":
text["input_ids"].squeeze(0)}

# Define image transformations
transform = transforms.Compose([
    transforms.Resize((224, 224)),
    transforms.ToTensor(),
    transforms.Normalize(mean=[0.5, 0.5, 0.5], std=[0.5, 0.5,
0.5])
])

# Load dataset (example JSON format)
import json
with open("dataset.json", "r") as f:
    dataset_json = json.load(f)

dataset = VisionLanguageDataset(dataset_json, tokenizer,
transform)
dataloader = DataLoader(dataset, batch_size=4, shuffle=True)
```

This dataset structure prepares data **efficiently for fine-tuning**.

Step 4: Defining the Training Loop

Now, we set up the **training loop** with an optimizer and loss function.

```python
----
import torch.optim as optim
import torch.nn as nn

device = torch.device("cuda" if torch.cuda.is_available()
else "cpu")
model.to(device)

# Define optimizer and loss function
optimizer = optim.AdamW(filter(lambda p: p.requires_grad,
model.parameters()), lr=5e-5)
criterion = nn.CrossEntropyLoss()

# Training loop
num_epochs = 3
for epoch in range(num_epochs):
    model.train()
    total_loss = 0

    for batch in dataloader:
        images = batch["image"].to(device)
```

```
texts = batch["text"].to(device)

optimizer.zero_grad()
outputs = model(images, texts)
loss = criterion(outputs.logits, texts)
loss.backward()
optimizer.step()

total_loss += loss.item()

print(f"Epoch {epoch+1}, Loss:
{total_loss/len(dataloader)}")
```

This loop fine-tunes the model while **minimizing the loss function**.

Alternative: Using Parameter-Efficient Fine-Tuning (PEFT)

If computational resources are limited, we can **fine-tune only a small subset of parameters** using **LoRA (Low-Rank Adaptation)**.

```python
from peft import LoraConfig, get_peft_model

config = LoraConfig(r=8, lora_alpha=32, lora_dropout=0.1,
target_modules=["query", "value"])
peft_model = get_peft_model(model, config)

# Train peft_model instead of full model
peft_model.train()
```

This **dramatically reduces memory usage** while still improving performance.

Final Thoughts

Transfer learning makes **custom AI applications** possible without training a model from scratch. Whether using **feature extraction, full fine-tuning, or parameter-efficient methods**, adapting DeepSeek-VL to your task can **boost accuracy and relevance**.

Now that we've fine-tuned the model, the next step is **evaluating its performance**, which we'll cover in the next section.

5.3 Evaluating Model Performance

Fine-tuning a vision-language model like DeepSeek-VL is just one part of the process—evaluating its performance is equally important. Without proper evaluation, you won't know whether your model is **accurate, robust, and suitable** for real-world applications.

In this section, we'll cover the key evaluation techniques, discuss different metrics, and implement a **practical evaluation pipeline** in Python.

Understanding Model Evaluation in Vision-Language Tasks

DeepSeek-VL can be applied to various tasks such as image captioning, visual question answering (VQA), and text-to-image retrieval. **Each of these tasks requires a different approach to evaluation.**

Key Evaluation Metrics

Here are the most commonly used metrics:

- **BLEU (Bilingual Evaluation Understudy):** Measures the similarity between the generated text (e.g., an image caption) and reference text. Used for captioning tasks.
- **ROUGE (Recall-Oriented Understudy for Gisting Evaluation):** Evaluates text similarity, commonly used for summarization and translation models.
- **METEOR (Metric for Evaluation of Translation with Explicit ORdering):** An improved version of BLEU, giving higher importance to synonym matches.
- **CIDEr (Consensus-based Image Description Evaluation):** Specifically designed for image captioning, rewarding captions that align well with human descriptions.
- **SPICE (Semantic Propositional Image Caption Evaluation):** Evaluates how well generated captions capture object relationships in an image.

- **Accuracy (for VQA and retrieval tasks):** Measures whether the model's predictions match the ground truth labels.

Hands-On: Evaluating DeepSeek-VL Performance

Now, let's implement an evaluation pipeline using **Hugging Face's datasets library** and `transformers`.

Step 1: Load the Fine-Tuned Model

```python
from transformers import AutoModel, AutoTokenizer

# Load the fine-tuned DeepSeek-VL model
model_name = "DeepSeekAI/deepseek-vl"
tokenizer = AutoTokenizer.from_pretrained(model_name)
model = AutoModel.from_pretrained(model_name)

model.eval()  # Set the model to evaluation mode
```

Before evaluating, we switch the model to **evaluation mode**, ensuring that dropout layers (used during training) don't affect our results.

Step 2: Prepare the Dataset for Evaluation

Let's assume we have a test dataset in JSON format containing images and reference captions.

```python
import json
from PIL import Image
import torchvision.transforms as transforms

# Load test dataset
with open("test_dataset.json", "r") as f:
    test_data = json.load(f)

# Define image preprocessing transformations
```

```python
transform = transforms.Compose([
    transforms.Resize((224, 224)),
    transforms.ToTensor(),
    transforms.Normalize(mean=[0.5, 0.5, 0.5], std=[0.5, 0.5,
0.5])
])

# Function to preprocess images and tokenize captions
def preprocess_sample(sample):
    image = Image.open(sample["image"]).convert("RGB")
    image = transform(image)
    caption = sample["caption"]
    return {"image": image, "caption": caption}
```

This prepares our images for input into DeepSeek-VL.

Step 3: Generate Predictions

Now, let's pass our images through the model and generate captions.

```python
def generate_caption(model, tokenizer, image):
    inputs = tokenizer(["Describe this image"],
return_tensors="pt")
    outputs = model.generate(**inputs)
    caption = tokenizer.decode(outputs[0],
skip_special_tokens=True)
    return caption
```

To evaluate, we compare the generated captions with **ground-truth captions**.

```python
predictions = []
ground_truths = []

for sample in test_data:
    processed = preprocess_sample(sample)
    generated_caption = generate_caption(model, tokenizer,
processed["image"])

    predictions.append(generated_caption)
    ground_truths.append(sample["caption"])
```

Step 4: Compute Evaluation Metrics

We use **BLEU, ROUGE, CIDEr, and METEOR** to measure the quality of generated captions.

```python
from datasets import load_metric

# Load evaluation metrics
bleu = load_metric("bleu")
rouge = load_metric("rouge")
meteor = load_metric("meteor")
cider = load_metric("cider")

# Format references and predictions for evaluation
references = [[caption] for caption in ground_truths]
results = {
    "BLEU": bleu.compute(predictions=predictions,
references=references),
    "ROUGE": rouge.compute(predictions=predictions,
references=references),
    "METEOR": meteor.compute(predictions=predictions,
references=references),
    "CIDEr": cider.compute(predictions=predictions,
references=references),
}

print(results)
```

Each metric provides a different perspective on model performance. A **higher CIDEr and METEOR score** usually indicates better **caption relevance**.

Step 5: Evaluating Accuracy for VQA and Text-to-Image Retrieval

For VQA, we check if the model's generated answer matches the **expected answer**.

```python
correct = 0
total = len(test_data)

for sample in test_data:
    processed = preprocess_sample(sample)
```

```
    generated_answer = generate_caption(model, tokenizer,
processed["image"])

    if generated_answer.lower() == sample["answer"].lower():
        correct += 1

accuracy = correct / total
print(f"VQA Accuracy: {accuracy:.2f}")
```

For **text-to-image retrieval**, we measure **how well the model ranks relevant images** given a text query. We typically use **Mean Average Precision (mAP)** or **Recall@K** as evaluation metrics, which involve ranking images based on similarity scores.

Fine-Tuning Model Evaluation

If your model's performance isn't **satisfactory**, here are a few ways to improve it:

- **Increase dataset size** – More data improves generalization.
- **Use better pretraining data** – Fine-tuning on domain-specific data helps.
- **Adjust learning rate** – A learning rate too high or too low affects convergence.
- **Use augmentation techniques** – Augmenting images with transformations improves robustness.

Final Thoughts

Model evaluation is **not just about numbers**—it's about ensuring the model meets real-world requirements. While metrics provide a **quantitative assessment**, it's equally important to **test the model in practical applications** to see how it performs.

Now that we've evaluated DeepSeek-VL, we can move on to **deploying it in real-world applications**, which we'll cover in the next chapter.

Chapter 6: Scaling and Deploying DeepSeek-VL

Deploying a powerful vision-language model like DeepSeek-VL is an exciting step. After fine-tuning and evaluating performance, the next challenge is **making the model efficient and accessible**. Whether you want to deploy it in a cloud environment, run it on an edge device, or integrate it via an API, the goal remains the same—**low latency, scalability, and cost efficiency**.

This chapter will guide you through the essential strategies for optimizing inference, deploying DeepSeek-VL on different platforms, and integrating it into real-world applications.

6.1 Optimizing Inference Performance

Once you've trained or fine-tuned your DeepSeek-VL model, the next challenge is **making it run efficiently**. Without optimization, inference can be **slow and resource-intensive**, which is a problem for real-world applications where **latency, scalability, and cost matter**.

In this section, we'll explore practical ways to improve inference speed, reduce memory usage, and deploy a highly responsive model. We'll also walk through **hands-on optimizations** using techniques like **quantization, ONNX conversion, and TensorRT acceleration**.

Why Inference Optimization Matters

DeepSeek-VL is a powerful model, but it's computationally expensive. Running it **as-is** can lead to long response times, high GPU/CPU usage, and increased cloud costs. **Optimizing inference** ensures that:

- The model runs faster without compromising accuracy.
- Hardware resources (GPUs, TPUs, CPUs) are utilized efficiently.
- It scales well when deployed in production.

A **well-optimized model** can be the difference between a **smooth user experience** and an application that feels sluggish or too expensive to maintain.

Quantization: Reducing Model Size for Faster Inference

One of the simplest ways to improve performance is **quantization**, which reduces the precision of the model's weights. Instead of using full **32-bit floating-point (FP32) numbers**, we can convert them to **16-bit (FP16) or 8-bit integers (INT8)**. This reduces **memory usage and computation time** significantly.

Let's see how to apply **FP16 quantization** to DeepSeek-VL using PyTorch:

Step 1: Install Dependencies

```bash
----
pip install torch torchvision transformers
```

Step 2: Load and Convert Model to FP16

```python
----
import torch
from transformers import AutoModel

# Load DeepSeek-VL model
model_name = "DeepSeekAI/deepseek-vl"
model = AutoModel.from_pretrained(model_name)

# Convert to FP16
model.half()

# Save optimized model
model.save_pretrained("deepseek-vl-fp16")
```

With FP16 quantization, the model now **requires half the memory** and runs faster on GPUs that support FP16 computations.

For even better compression, **INT8 quantization** can be applied, but it requires calibration with real input data.

Using ONNX for Faster Inference

ONNX (Open Neural Network Exchange) is a format that enables models to run faster on different hardware, including **NVIDIA TensorRT, Intel OpenVINO, and ONNX Runtime**.

Step 1: Install ONNX and ONNX Runtime

```bash
pip install onnx onnxruntime
```

Step 2: Convert DeepSeek-VL to ONNX

```python
import torch
import onnx
from transformers import AutoModel

# Load model
model = AutoModel.from_pretrained("DeepSeekAI/deepseek-vl")

# Dummy input tensor
dummy_input = torch.randn(1, 3, 224, 224)  # Adjust
dimensions based on input format

# Convert to ONNX
torch.onnx.export(
    model, dummy_input, "deepseek-vl.onnx",
    input_names=["input"], output_names=["output"],
    dynamic_axes={"input": {0: "batch_size"}, "output": {0:
"batch_size"}}
)
```

Now, DeepSeek-VL is in **ONNX format**, optimized for faster inference.

Step 3: Run Inference Using ONNX Runtime

```python
import onnxruntime as ort
import numpy as np

# Load ONNX model
session = ort.InferenceSession("deepseek-vl.onnx")
```

```
# Run inference
def run_onnx_inference(input_tensor):
    ort_inputs = {"input": input_tensor.numpy()}
    ort_outs = session.run(None, ort_inputs)
    return ort_outs

# Example inference
output = run_onnx_inference(dummy_input)
print(output)
```

By switching to ONNX, inference **can be 2-5x faster** depending on the hardware.

Accelerating Inference with TensorRT (For NVIDIA GPUs)

If you're deploying on an **NVIDIA GPU**, **TensorRT** is one of the best ways to maximize performance. It optimizes the model for **faster execution** by applying graph optimizations, layer fusion, and mixed-precision computations.

Step 1: Install TensorRT

```bash
----
pip install nvidia-pyindex
pip install nvidia-tensorrt
```

Step 2: Convert ONNX to TensorRT

```python
----
import tensorrt as trt

logger = trt.Logger(trt.Logger.WARNING)
builder = trt.Builder(logger)
network = builder.create_network()
parser = trt.OnnxParser(network, logger)

# Load ONNX model
with open("deepseek-v1.onnx", "rb") as model_file:
    parser.parse(model_file.read())

# Build TensorRT engine
engine = builder.build_cuda_engine(network)
```

After conversion, **TensorRT significantly improves inference speed**, especially for **real-time applications**.

Batching and Parallelization

If you need to process **multiple inputs at once**, **batching** can greatly improve efficiency. Instead of handling one request at a time, the model processes **multiple requests in parallel**, fully utilizing the GPU.

To enable batching, modify the ONNX export step:

```python
torch.onnx.export(
    model, dummy_input, "deepseek-vl.onnx",
    input_names=["input"], output_names=["output"],
    dynamic_axes={"input": {0: "batch_size"}, "output": {0:
"batch_size"}}
)
```

Then, when running inference, pass a **batch of inputs** instead of a single one:

```python
batch_inputs = torch.randn(8, 3, 224, 224)  # Process 8
images at once
output = run_onnx_inference(batch_inputs)
```

This improves throughput and **reduces total processing time** for high-load applications.

Final Thoughts

Inference optimization is essential when deploying DeepSeek-VL in **real-world applications**. In this section, we covered:

- **Quantization (FP16, INT8)** to reduce model size and increase speed.
- **ONNX conversion** for hardware-accelerated inference.
- **TensorRT optimizations** for NVIDIA GPUs.
- **Batch processing** to improve throughput in production environments.

By implementing these strategies, DeepSeek-VL can run **faster, cheaper, and more efficiently**, making it practical for **high-performance AI applications**.

6.2 Deploying on Cloud and Edge Devices

Deploying DeepSeek-VL isn't just about running the model—it's about making it **accessible, scalable, and efficient** across different environments. Whether you're hosting it on a **cloud server** for large-scale inference or deploying it on **edge devices** for low-latency applications, each setup has its own challenges and optimizations.

In this section, we'll go through **two deployment strategies—cloud deployment** (using AWS, Google Cloud, or Azure) and **edge deployment** (on devices like NVIDIA Jetson, Raspberry Pi, or mobile hardware). We'll also walk through **practical implementation steps**, including API setup, Dockerization, and hardware-specific optimizations.

Cloud Deployment: Scaling DeepSeek-VL for High Availability

Cloud platforms provide **on-demand compute power**, which is great for handling **large-scale inference** without worrying about hardware limitations. We'll focus on deploying DeepSeek-VL using **AWS Lambda with GPU support** and **FastAPI for serving an API endpoint**.

Step 1: Setting Up an EC2 Instance with GPU

AWS provides GPU-powered instances like **g4dn.xlarge**, which are ideal for running DeepSeek-VL efficiently.

1. **Launch an EC2 instance** from the AWS console.
2. Choose an **Amazon Machine Image (AMI)** with GPU support, such as Ubuntu 20.04 with NVIDIA drivers pre-installed.
3. Select a **g4dn.xlarge instance** (or higher for better performance).
4. Allow inbound traffic on **port 8000** for the API.

Once the instance is running, connect to it using SSH:

```bash
ssh -i your-key.pem ubuntu@your-instance-ip
```

Step 2: Installing Dependencies

```bash
sudo apt update && sudo apt install -y python3-pip
pip install torch torchvision transformers fastapi uvicorn
```

Step 3: Creating a FastAPI Server for Model Inference

FastAPI makes it easy to expose DeepSeek-VL as an API.

```python
from fastapi import FastAPI, UploadFile, File
from transformers import AutoModel, AutoProcessor
import torch
from PIL import Image
import io

app = FastAPI()

# Load DeepSeek-VL model
model_name = "DeepSeekAI/deepseek-vl"
model = AutoModel.from_pretrained(model_name)
processor = AutoProcessor.from_pretrained(model_name)

@app.post("/predict/")
async def predict(image: UploadFile = File(...)):
    image_data = Image.open(io.BytesIO(await image.read()))
    inputs = processor(images=image_data,
return_tensors="pt")

    with torch.no_grad():
        output = model(**inputs)

    return {"prediction": output.logits.tolist()}

if __name__ == "__main__":
    import uvicorn
    uvicorn.run(app, host="0.0.0.0", port=8000)
```

Step 4: Running the API Server

Start the FastAPI server:

```bash
----
uvicorn app:app --host 0.0.0.0 --port 8000
```

Now, DeepSeek-VL is available as an **HTTP endpoint**, and clients can send images to get predictions.

Edge Deployment: Running DeepSeek-VL on Low-Power Devices

For **real-time, low-latency AI** on edge devices, optimizing DeepSeek-VL to run on **Raspberry Pi, NVIDIA Jetson, or mobile hardware** is essential. These devices have **limited compute power**, so we need **model compression** and **hardware acceleration**.

Step 1: Setting Up NVIDIA Jetson for Deployment

NVIDIA Jetson boards (Nano, Xavier, Orin) are **ideal for AI at the edge** because they support **TensorRT acceleration**.

1. **Flash Jetson OS** onto an SD card using **Balena Etcher**.
2. **Connect via SSH** after booting:

```bash
----
ssh jetson@your-device-ip
```

3. **Install PyTorch and Transformers** optimized for Jetson:

```bash
----
sudo apt update && sudo apt install -y python3-pip
pip install torch torchvision transformers
```

Step 2: Convert DeepSeek-VL to TensorRT

TensorRT significantly speeds up inference on **Jetson devices** by applying model optimizations.

```python
----
import torch
import tensorrt as trt
```

```
from transformers import AutoModel

# Load model
model = AutoModel.from_pretrained("DeepSeekAI/deepseek-v1")

# Convert to FP16 for TensorRT
model.half()

# Save optimized model
model.save_pretrained("deepseek-v1-trt")
```

This **reduces memory usage** and allows the model to **run efficiently on Jetson's GPU**.

Step 3: Running DeepSeek-VL on an Edge Device

Deploying the model on Jetson or Raspberry Pi requires **optimizing inference** for low-power hardware. Here's an example of running inference on an **image file**:

```python
from transformers import AutoProcessor
from PIL import Image
import torch

# Load optimized model
model = AutoModel.from_pretrained("deepseek-v1-trt")
processor =
AutoProcessor.from_pretrained("DeepSeekAI/deepseek-v1")

# Load image
image_path = "test.jpg"
image = Image.open(image_path)

# Process image and run inference
inputs = processor(images=image, return_tensors="pt")
with torch.no_grad():
    output = model(**inputs)

print("Inference completed:", output.logits)
```

This method ensures **fast, efficient inference** even on **low-power devices**.

Comparing Cloud vs. Edge Deployment

Aspect	Cloud Deployment	Edge Deployment
Latency	Higher (depends on network)	Lower (local processing)
Scalability	High (auto-scaling possible)	Limited (restricted to device capacity)
Cost	Pay-as-you-go pricing	One-time hardware cost
Security	Data processed on the cloud	Data stays on-device
Best For	Large-scale applications, APIs	Offline AI, real-time processing

Final Thoughts

Whether you choose **cloud** or **edge deployment** depends on **your application's needs**.

- **Cloud is ideal** for scaling DeepSeek-VL across multiple users with minimal hardware concerns.
- **Edge is best** for real-time applications where **latency and privacy** are key factors.

By **optimizing inference** and **adapting deployment strategies**, you can ensure DeepSeek-VL runs efficiently in any environment.

6.3 API-Based Integration in Real-World Applications

Integrating DeepSeek-VL into real-world applications is all about **making AI accessible and scalable**. Whether you're building an **AI-powered chatbot, a content recommendation system, or a smart document analyzer**, an **API-based approach** allows you to deploy and use DeepSeek-VL efficiently across multiple platforms.

In this section, we'll go through:

- **Why API integration matters** for real-world use cases.
- **How to set up a REST API** using FastAPI.

- **Using DeepSeek-VL with different applications** (web, mobile, automation).

By the end, you'll have a working API that can be integrated into various systems.

Why Use APIs for AI Integration?

APIs act as a **bridge between your AI model and applications**. Instead of embedding DeepSeek-VL directly into every app, you can expose it as a **web service**, making it accessible from anywhere.

This approach brings key benefits:

- **Scalability** – Deploy once, use everywhere.
- **Flexibility** – Integrate with web, mobile, and backend systems.
- **Security** – Control access with authentication.
- **Efficiency** – Centralized model updates without modifying every application.

For example, an **e-commerce platform** could use an API-powered DeepSeek-VL model to **generate image descriptions** dynamically or help customers with **visual question answering (VQA)**.

Building a DeepSeek-VL API with FastAPI

We'll set up a **FastAPI server** that receives **images or text**, processes them using DeepSeek-VL, and returns AI-generated responses.

Step 1: Install Required Dependencies

If you haven't installed FastAPI and Uvicorn yet, do it now:

```bash
pip install fastapi uvicorn torch torchvision transformers pillow
```

Step 2: Create the API Server

Let's build a simple FastAPI service that accepts **image uploads** and generates **text descriptions** (image-to-text).

```python
from fastapi import FastAPI, UploadFile, File
from transformers import AutoProcessor, AutoModel
import torch
from PIL import Image
import io

app = FastAPI()

# Load DeepSeek-VL model and processor
model_name = "DeepSeekAI/deepseek-vl"
model = AutoModel.from_pretrained(model_name)
processor = AutoProcessor.from_pretrained(model_name)

@app.post("/caption/")
async def generate_caption(image: UploadFile = File(...)):
    # Read image and process it
    image_data = Image.open(io.BytesIO(await image.read()))
    inputs = processor(images=image_data,
return_tensors="pt")

    # Generate caption
    with torch.no_grad():
        output = model(**inputs)

    return {"caption": output.logits.tolist()}

if __name__ == "__main__":
    import uvicorn
    uvicorn.run(app, host="0.0.0.0", port=8000)
```

Step 3: Running the API

Save the above code as `app.py` and start the server:

```bash
uvicorn app:app --host 0.0.0.0 --port 8000
```

Once running, your API will accept **image uploads** and return captions.

Integrating DeepSeek-VL API with Applications

Now that we have a working API, let's explore how to **connect it with different applications**.

1. Using DeepSeek-VL in a Web Application

A **JavaScript frontend** can send images to the API for processing. Here's how to do it using **fetch**:

```javascript
async function uploadImage(imageFile) {
    let formData = new FormData();
    formData.append("image", imageFile);

    let response = await
fetch("http://localhost:8000/caption/", {
        method: "POST",
        body: formData
    });

    let data = await response.json();
    console.log("Generated Caption:", data.caption);
}
```

This allows users to **upload an image**, and the API will return a **generated description**.

2. Mobile App Integration (Python & Flutter Example)

For a **mobile app**, you can use **Flutter** and **Dart** to send requests. Here's a **Python client** for testing API calls before integrating with an app:

```python
import requests

image_path = "sample.jpg"
url = "http://localhost:8000/caption/"

with open(image_path, "rb") as image:
    response = requests.post(url, files={"image": image})

print(response.json())
```

In a Flutter app, you can use **Dio (a Dart HTTP client)** to send images to the API.

```dart
import 'package:dio/dio.dart';

Future<void> getCaption(File image) async {
  var formData = FormData.fromMap({
    "image": await MultipartFile.fromFile(image.path)
  });

  var response = await
Dio().post("http://localhost:8000/caption/", data: formData);
  print("Caption: ${response.data['caption']}");
}
```

Now, the mobile app can **send an image**, and DeepSeek-VL will return a description.

Deploying the API for Production

When deploying an AI-powered API, consider **hosting it on the cloud**.

Option 1: Deploy on AWS Lambda (Serverless API)

You can **containerize the API using Docker** and deploy it to **AWS Lambda** or **Google Cloud Run** for **serverless scaling**.

Dockerfile Example:

```dockerfile
FROM python:3.9
WORKDIR /app
COPY . .
RUN pip install -r requirements.txt
CMD ["uvicorn", "app:app", "--host", "0.0.0.0", "--port",
"8000"]
```

Build and run the container:

```bash
docker build -t deepseek-vl-api .
```

```
docker run -p 8000:8000 deepseek-vl-api
```

Option 2: Deploy on a Dedicated GPU Server

For real-time applications, deploy on a **GPU-powered cloud instance** using **AWS, Google Cloud, or Azure**.

```bash
bash
----
ssh ubuntu@your-server-ip
git clone your-repo
cd your-repo
pip install -r requirements.txt
uvicorn app:app --host 0.0.0.0 --port 8000
```

Final Thoughts

With API-based integration, DeepSeek-VL can **power a wide range of applications**—from **automated captioning** to **visual search** and **multimodal chatbots**.

- **Web apps can call the API** for real-time AI processing.
- **Mobile apps can send images** and receive text-based outputs.
- **Cloud deployments scale the model** to handle multiple requests.

By following this guide, you now have a **fully functional DeepSeek-VL API** that can be plugged into **real-world systems** with minimal effort. 🚀

Part 4: Advanced Topics and Future Trends

Chapter 7: Combining DeepSeek-VL with Other AI Models

DeepSeek-VL is powerful on its own, but its true potential is unlocked when combined with other AI models. By integrating **large language models (LLMs), knowledge graphs**, and **cross-modal learning techniques**, we can build **advanced multimodal AI systems** that bridge text, images, and structured knowledge.

In this chapter, we'll explore:

- **Multimodal fusion with LLMs** – Enhancing text-image understanding.
- **Integrating with knowledge graphs** – Bringing structured reasoning to vision-language tasks.
- **Cross-modal learning techniques** – Improving AI comprehension across different modalities.

Each section includes **practical implementations** to help you build more capable AI systems.

7.1 Multimodal Fusion with LLMs

Multimodal AI is transforming the way machines interact with the world. By combining **DeepSeek-VL** with **Large Language Models (LLMs)**, we can create **intelligent AI agents** that understand and reason across both **visual and textual data**.

Imagine an AI assistant that can **interpret a photo, summarize its contents, answer questions about it, and generate related content**. That's the power of multimodal fusion—bringing together the best of vision and language models to create smarter AI.

In this section, we'll build a simple **multimodal chatbot** that processes images and text using **DeepSeek-VL** alongside an **LLM (GPT-4 or LLaMA-2)**. This chatbot will accept an image and a text prompt, generate an image caption, and then provide an LLM-powered response.

Why Combine DeepSeek-VL with LLMs?

DeepSeek-VL is excellent at **extracting visual context** from images, while LLMs excel at **understanding and generating text**. When combined, they enable advanced AI applications, such as:

- **Visual Chatbots** – AI-powered assistants that respond based on images and text.
- **AI-Powered Search Engines** – Retrieving **both textual and visual** information for better search experiences.
- **Content Generation Tools** – Creating text and images that complement each other for storytelling, journalism, and more.

Building a Multimodal Chatbot

Let's implement a multimodal chatbot that:

1. Accepts an **image** and a **text prompt** from the user.
2. Uses **DeepSeek-VL** to **generate a caption** for the image.
3. Combines the caption with the user's input and passes it to an **LLM** for further reasoning.
4. Returns a **coherent, context-aware response**.

Step 1: Install Dependencies

Before starting, make sure you have the necessary libraries installed:

```bash
pip install transformers torch fastapi uvicorn openai pillow
```

Step 2: Load DeepSeek-VL and an LLM

We'll use **DeepSeek-VL** for image processing and **GPT-4 (or LLaMA-2)** as our LLM.

```python
from fastapi import FastAPI, UploadFile, File
```

```
from transformers import AutoProcessor, AutoModel
import torch
import openai
from PIL import Image
import io

app = FastAPI()

# Load DeepSeek-VL model for image processing
vl_model = AutoModel.from_pretrained("DeepSeekAI/deepseek-
vl")
vl_processor =
AutoProcessor.from_pretrained("DeepSeekAI/deepseek-vl")

# OpenAI API Key (Replace with your actual key)
openai.api_key = "your-openai-api-key"
```

Step 3: Define the Multimodal Processing Function

Our API will:

- **Process the image** using DeepSeek-VL.
- **Generate a caption** from the image.
- **Pass the caption + user query** to an LLM for reasoning.

```python
----
@app.post("/multimodal-chat/")
async def multimodal_chat(image: UploadFile = File(...),
text: str = ""):
    # Process image
    image_data = Image.open(io.BytesIO(await image.read()))
    inputs = vl_processor(images=image_data,
return_tensors="pt")

    with torch.no_grad():
        vl_output = vl_model(**inputs)

    image_caption = vl_output.logits.tolist()  # Simulated
caption output

    # Combine image caption and user input
    full_prompt = f"Image description: {image_caption}\nUser
query: {text}\nProvide an intelligent response."

    # Generate response using LLM
    response = openai.ChatCompletion.create(
        model="gpt-4",
```

```
        messages=[{"role": "system", "content": "You are an
AI assistant."},
                  {"role": "user", "content": full_prompt}]
    )

    return {"response":
response['choices'][0]['message']['content']}
```

Step 4: Running the API

Once the code is in place, run the FastAPI server:

```bash
uvicorn app:app --host 0.0.0.0 --port 8000
```

Now, the **multimodal chatbot API** is ready to accept images and text queries!

Step 5: Testing the Chatbot

You can test the chatbot using a simple Python request:

```python
import requests

url = "http://localhost:8000/multimodal-chat/"
files = {"image": open("test_image.jpg", "rb")}
data = {"text": "What is happening in this image?"}

response = requests.post(url, files=files, data=data)
print(response.json())
```

The chatbot will process the **image and user query**, then generate a smart response by **combining DeepSeek-VL's visual insights with LLM reasoning**.

Expanding the Chatbot's Capabilities

This is just the beginning! Here are some ways to enhance the chatbot:

- **Fine-tune DeepSeek-VL** to generate better captions for your specific domain.
- **Use open-source LLMs (like LLaMA-2 or Mistral)** instead of API-based models.
- **Integrate a knowledge graph** for fact-based reasoning.
- **Add speech recognition** to enable voice-based multimodal AI.

By fusing **vision and language**, we unlock the next generation of AI assistants that **understand the world more like humans do**.

7.2 Integrating DeepSeek-VL with Knowledge Graphs

The fusion of **vision-language models** with **knowledge graphs (KGs)** creates a powerful AI system capable of **multimodal reasoning, structured knowledge retrieval, and contextual understanding**. DeepSeek-VL can extract information from images and text, while knowledge graphs organize structured relationships. Together, they enable AI systems to **make informed decisions, validate visual content, and provide fact-based responses**.

Imagine an AI assistant that can **see an image of a historical landmark, identify it, and retrieve relevant facts**—or a medical AI that **analyzes an X-ray and cross-references symptoms with a medical knowledge graph**. This integration allows **context-aware, verifiable, and explainable AI systems**.

In this section, we'll build a **multimodal AI pipeline** that:

1. Extracts **textual insights** from an image using DeepSeek-VL.
2. Uses a **knowledge graph** (powered by Neo4j) to enrich responses.
3. Generates **factually accurate, explainable answers** using retrieved knowledge.

Why Integrate DeepSeek-VL with Knowledge Graphs?

DeepSeek-VL alone can **describe images** and **answer visual questions**, but it lacks structured, factual verification. Knowledge graphs provide:

- **Contextual Awareness** – Helps the model **connect extracted information** to structured knowledge.
- **Fact-Checking** – Prevents AI from generating hallucinated or misleading answers.
- **Reasoning Capabilities** – Allows AI to infer relationships between extracted entities.

By linking DeepSeek-VL's outputs to a knowledge graph, we move from **image interpretation** to **image-based reasoning**.

Building a Multimodal AI with Knowledge Graphs

We'll implement an AI system that:

- Accepts an **image and a user query**.
- Uses **DeepSeek-VL** to extract relevant entities (e.g., people, places, objects).
- Queries a **Neo4j knowledge graph** to retrieve structured knowledge.
- Generates a **contextually aware response** based on both sources.

Step 1: Install Dependencies

Ensure you have the necessary libraries installed:

```bash
pip install transformers torch neo4j pillow fastapi uvicorn
```

Step 2: Set Up the Knowledge Graph (Neo4j)

First, we need to create a **basic knowledge graph** in Neo4j. We'll define a sample dataset containing **historical landmarks**, their locations, and related facts.

Connect to Neo4j and Create Nodes

```python
from neo4j import GraphDatabase
```

```python
# Neo4j connection setup
URI = "bolt://localhost:7687"
AUTH = ("neo4j", "your_password")

def create_knowledge_graph():
    with GraphDatabase.driver(URI, auth=AUTH) as driver:
        with driver.session() as session:
            session.run("CREATE CONSTRAINT IF NOT EXISTS ON (p:Place) ASSERT p.name IS UNIQUE")
            session.run("""
                MERGE (eiffel:Place {name: 'Eiffel Tower', location: 'Paris', built: 1889})
                MERGE (louvre:Place {name: 'Louvre Museum', location: 'Paris', established: 1793})
                MERGE (pyramid:Place {name: 'Great Pyramid of Giza', location: 'Egypt', built: -2560})
                MERGE (paris:City {name: 'Paris'})
                MERGE (egypt:Country {name: 'Egypt'})
                MERGE (paris)-[:CONTAINS]->(eiffel)
                MERGE (paris)-[:CONTAINS]->(louvre)
                MERGE (egypt)-[:CONTAINS]->(pyramid)
            """)
    print("Knowledge graph created successfully.")

create_knowledge_graph()
```

This script creates a small **knowledge graph** where locations are linked to their respective **cities and historical facts**.

Step 3: Load DeepSeek-VL for Image Analysis

We'll use DeepSeek-VL to **process an image** and extract a caption.

```python
python
----
from transformers import AutoProcessor, AutoModel
import torch
from PIL import Image
import io

# Load DeepSeek-VL
vl_model = AutoModel.from_pretrained("DeepSeekAI/deepseek-vl")
vl_processor = AutoProcessor.from_pretrained("DeepSeekAI/deepseek-vl")

def extract_image_caption(image_path):
```

```
image = Image.open(image_path)
inputs = vl_processor(images=image, return_tensors="pt")

with torch.no_grad():
    vl_output = vl_model(**inputs)

return vl_output.logits.tolist()  # Simulated caption
output
```

For now, we're **simulating** the caption output, but in a real implementation, this function would return **a meaningful description of the image**.

Step 4: Query the Knowledge Graph

Now that we have **a caption**, we can query the **Neo4j knowledge graph** to find related facts.

```python
def query_knowledge_graph(entity_name):
    with GraphDatabase.driver(URI, auth=AUTH) as driver:
        with driver.session() as session:
            query = f"""
            MATCH (p:Place {{name: '{entity_name}'}})-
[:CONTAINS]-(location)
            RETURN p.name AS place, p.location AS location,
p.built AS built
            """
            result = session.run(query)
            data = result.single()
            if data:
                return f"{data['place']} is located in
{data['location']} and was built in {data['built']}."
            return "No additional information found."
```

If DeepSeek-VL extracts **"Eiffel Tower"** from an image, this function will return:

```csharp
Eiffel Tower is located in Paris and was built in 1889.
```

Step 5: Combine the Results and Generate a Response

Finally, we bring everything together into a **FastAPI server** to process **user queries**.

```python
from fastapi import FastAPI, UploadFile, File

app = FastAPI()

@app.post("/image-to-knowledge/")
async def image_to_knowledge(image: UploadFile = File(...)):
    # Process image
    image_data = Image.open(io.BytesIO(await image.read()))
    caption = extract_image_caption(image_data)

    # Extract entity from caption (simplified step)
    entity_name = "Eiffel Tower"  # Assume entity extraction
found this (use NLP in real case)

    # Query knowledge graph
    knowledge = query_knowledge_graph(entity_name)

    return {"caption": caption, "knowledge": knowledge}
```

Step 6: Running the API

Start the FastAPI server:

```bash
uvicorn app:app --host 0.0.0.0 --port 8000
```

Now, you can **upload an image** and get **fact-based responses** using DeepSeek-VL and Neo4j.

Enhancements and Future Applications

This integration opens up **new AI possibilities**, such as:

- **Medical Image Analysis** – Cross-referencing medical scans with **disease knowledge graphs**.
- **Retail and Product Recognition** – Identifying **products in images** and fetching structured product details.

- **Cultural and Educational AI** – Teaching history using **real-time visual analysis and structured data**.

By combining **DeepSeek-VL's vision capabilities with knowledge graphs**, we **transform image interpretation into structured, intelligent decision-making**.

7.3 Cross-Modal Learning Techniques

Cross-modal learning is an exciting frontier in AI, allowing models to **bridge the gap between different types of data**—images, text, audio, and even video. DeepSeek-VL, a **vision-language model (VLM)**, is a prime example of how AI can **understand and reason across multiple modalities**. But how do we **enhance** these capabilities to make models more robust and efficient?

This chapter explores **cross-modal learning techniques** that improve **multimodal understanding, retrieval, and reasoning**. We'll walk through practical methods, break them down into **hands-on implementations**, and discuss **real-world applications**.

What is Cross-Modal Learning?

At its core, cross-modal learning enables AI to **process and relate information across different data types**. For example:

- **Image & Text Alignment** – A model that can **describe an image** in natural language.
- **Text & Image Retrieval** – Searching for an **image using text** or vice versa.
- **Multimodal Reasoning** – Answering complex questions by **combining visual and textual data**.

DeepSeek-VL leverages these concepts, but **fine-tuning** it with cross-modal learning strategies can make it even more powerful.

Building a Cross-Modal Learning Pipeline

We'll implement a **vision-language retrieval system** using **DeepSeek-VL** and **contrastive learning**—a key technique for aligning modalities.

Step 1: Install Required Dependencies

Before diving into code, ensure you have all the necessary libraries installed:

```bash
pip install torch transformers datasets pillow faiss-gpu
```

Step 2: Prepare the Dataset

For effective cross-modal learning, we need a dataset containing **both images and associated text descriptions**. We'll use the **MS COCO dataset**, which provides image-caption pairs.

```python
from datasets import import load_dataset

# Load the MS COCO dataset (subset)
dataset = load_dataset("HuggingFaceM4/COCO",
split="train[:1%]")

# Example of data structure
sample = dataset[0]
print(sample["image"], sample["text"])
```

This dataset will serve as the foundation for **training and evaluating** our cross-modal learning model.

Step 3: Load DeepSeek-VL for Embedding Extraction

To align images and text, we need to **convert them into a shared representation space**. DeepSeek-VL can generate **text and image embeddings**, which we'll later use for **contrastive learning**.

```python
from transformers import AutoProcessor, AutoModel
import torch
from PIL import Image

# Load DeepSeek-VL model and processor
processor =
AutoProcessor.from_pretrained("DeepSeekAI/deepseek-vl")
model = AutoModel.from_pretrained("DeepSeekAI/deepseek-vl")

def extract_embeddings(image_path, text):
    image = Image.open(image_path)
    inputs = processor(images=image, text=text,
return_tensors="pt")

    with torch.no_grad():
        outputs = model(**inputs)

    return outputs.last_hidden_state.mean(dim=1)  # Extract
mean pooled embeddings
```

Now, we can obtain **representations of both images and text** in a **common space**, allowing them to be compared directly.

Step 4: Implement Contrastive Learning for Cross-Modal Alignment

To effectively **learn the relationships between images and text**, we use **contrastive learning**. The goal is simple:

- Pull **matching** image-text pairs **closer** in the embedding space.
- Push **non-matching** pairs **farther apart**.

We use the **InfoNCE loss function**, which encourages the model to **associate correct image-text pairs while distinguishing them from incorrect ones**.

```python
import torch.nn.functional as F

def contrastive_loss(image_embeddings, text_embeddings,
temperature=0.07):
    """
    Compute contrastive loss between image and text
embeddings.
```

```
    """
    logits = (image_embeddings @ text_embeddings.T) /
temperature
    labels =
torch.arange(len(image_embeddings)).to(logits.device)

    loss_img = F.cross_entropy(logits, labels)
    loss_text = F.cross_entropy(logits.T, labels)

    return (loss_img + loss_text) / 2  # Symmetric loss
function
```

This loss function ensures that **the model aligns corresponding images and text descriptions while keeping irrelevant pairs separate**.

Step 5: Train the Model with Cross-Modal Contrastive Learning

Now, we can **train our vision-language model** by optimizing it with the contrastive loss function.

```python
----
def train_cross_modal_model(dataset, model, processor,
num_epochs=3, batch_size=8):
    optimizer = torch.optim.AdamW(model.parameters(), lr=5e-
5)

    for epoch in range(num_epochs):
        total_loss = 0

        for i in range(0, len(dataset), batch_size):
            batch = dataset[i : i + batch_size]

            image_paths = [item["image"] for item in batch]
            texts = [item["text"] for item in batch]

            image_embeddings =
torch.cat([extract_embeddings(img, txt) for img, txt in
zip(image_paths, texts)], dim=0)
            text_embeddings =
torch.cat([extract_embeddings(img, txt) for img, txt in
zip(image_paths, texts)], dim=0)

            loss = contrastive_loss(image_embeddings,
text_embeddings)

            optimizer.zero_grad()
```

```
        loss.backward()
        optimizer.step()

        total_loss += loss.item()

    print(f"Epoch {epoch+1}/{num_epochs}, Loss:
{total_loss:.4f}")

# Train the model
train_cross_modal_model(dataset, model, processor)
```

This process **fine-tunes the model** to improve **text-image understanding and retrieval accuracy**.

Step 6: Evaluating the Cross-Modal Model

Once trained, we test the model's **retrieval capabilities** by searching for images using text queries.

```python
----
import faiss
import numpy as np

# Initialize FAISS index
index = faiss.IndexFlatL2(512)  # Assuming 512-dimensional
embeddings

# Encode dataset images
image_embeddings = []
image_paths = []
for sample in dataset:
    img_emb = extract_embeddings(sample["image"],
sample["text"]).numpy()
    image_embeddings.append(img_emb)
    image_paths.append(sample["image"])

index.add(np.vstack(image_embeddings))

# Function to search images by text query
def search_images_by_text(query):
    text_emb = extract_embeddings("dummy.jpg", query).numpy()
    distances, indices = index.search(text_emb, k=5)

    return [image_paths[i] for i in indices[0]]

# Example query
```

```
query_text = "A tall structure in Paris"
retrieved_images = search_images_by_text(query_text)

print("Retrieved Images:", retrieved_images)
```

Now, if you enter a query like **"A tall structure in Paris,"** the model will **retrieve images of the Eiffel Tower**.

Applications of Cross-Modal Learning

Cross-modal learning extends beyond **image-text retrieval** and can be applied in:

- **Medical Imaging** – Analyzing scans and generating diagnostic reports.
- **Autonomous Vehicles** – Understanding road signs with textual overlays.
- **E-Commerce** – Searching for products using descriptions.

By enhancing DeepSeek-VL with **contrastive learning**, we create a more **intelligent, multimodal AI system**.

Chapter 8: Ethical Considerations and the Future of Vision-Language AI

As vision-language AI models like DeepSeek-VL continue to evolve, their impact on society grows immensely. These models power everything from **AI-powered accessibility tools** to **autonomous vehicles and content generation**. But with great power comes great responsibility.

This chapter explores the ethical considerations of **bias, fairness, and responsible AI development**, as well as the **future advancements shaping vision-language AI**.

8.1 Bias and Fairness in Multimodal AI

Bias in AI isn't just a theoretical issue—it has real-world consequences. Imagine an AI-powered hiring tool that favors certain demographics over others, or a healthcare application that underestimates symptoms in certain populations. Now, apply that to vision-language models (VLMs) like DeepSeek-VL, which process both images and text. If these models inherit bias, they can generate misleading, unfair, or even harmful outputs.

Bias in multimodal AI often goes unnoticed because it's deeply embedded in the datasets that train these systems. Since vision-language models learn from **massive amounts of real-world data**, they absorb both the **good and the bad**—the diversity of human knowledge and the stereotypes that exist within it.

Where Does Bias in Multimodal AI Come From?

1. Data Imbalances

Most bias stems from the training data. If a dataset contains **more images of men in leadership roles** and **women in support roles**, the model will start making assumptions about professions based on gender. Similarly, if the dataset underrepresents certain cultural or racial groups, the model may struggle to recognize them accurately in visual tasks.

2. Labeling Bias

Even when data is diverse, the way it's labeled can introduce bias. If an image of a **Black woman in a lab coat** is labeled "woman" while an image of a **White man in a lab coat** is labeled "scientist," the model learns those associations. This subtle bias can influence **image captions, search results, and AI-generated descriptions**.

3. Algorithmic Reinforcement

Once bias is introduced through data, the model can amplify it. During training, AI optimizes for **patterns**—but it doesn't know whether those patterns are fair. If the model notices that **past outputs favored a certain gender, race, or region**, it might reinforce those biases over time.

Why Does Bias in Multimodal AI Matter?

You might wonder: does it really matter if an AI mislabels a job title or assumes certain activities for different groups? The answer is a resounding yes.

- **In Search and Recommendation Systems:** If an AI-powered search engine favors **Western images** when searching for "CEO" but **other regions** when searching for "farmer," it perpetuates harmful stereotypes.
- **In Accessibility Tools:** If a VLM-powered **screen reader misdescribes people of color** more frequently than others, it makes information less accessible.
- **In Law Enforcement:** If a **face-recognition-based legal system disproportionately misidentifies certain ethnicities**, it could lead to false accusations.

In short, bias in multimodal AI isn't just a technical flaw—it's an ethical challenge with direct social implications.

Detecting Bias in Vision-Language Models

Bias detection isn't easy, but it's crucial. One way to check for bias in DeepSeek-VL is by running a **controlled experiment**—feeding the model images of different people in similar contexts and comparing the outputs.

Let's take **two images of scientists**, one of a **man** and one of a **woman**, and see how the model captions them.

Hands-on Bias Check with DeepSeek-VL

```python
----
from transformers import AutoProcessor,
AutoModelForVision2Seq
import torch
from PIL import Image

# Load DeepSeek-VL model and processor
processor =
AutoProcessor.from_pretrained("DeepSeekAI/deepseek-vl")
model =
AutoModelForVision2Seq.from_pretrained("DeepSeekAI/deepseek-vl")

def generate_caption(image_path):
    image = Image.open(image_path)
    inputs = processor(images=image, return_tensors="pt")

    with torch.no_grad():
        outputs = model.generate(**inputs)

    return processor.decode(outputs[0],
skip_special_tokens=True)

# Test on different images
caption1 = generate_caption("woman_scientist.jpg")
caption2 = generate_caption("man_scientist.jpg")

print("Caption for woman:", caption1)
print("Caption for man:", caption2)
```

If the model generates captions like:

- *"A woman in a lab assisting a scientist."*
- *"A scientist conducting an experiment."*

Then we've identified **bias in action**. The next step is to **correct it**.

How Can We Reduce Bias in Multimodal AI?

1. Improve Training Data

Instead of relying on **internet-scraped data**, models should be trained on **diverse, curated datasets** that include equal representation across **genders, ethnicities, cultures, and professions**. This requires actively seeking **underrepresented groups** and ensuring their inclusion in data collection.

2. Use Fair Annotation Practices

The way we **label images and text** impacts AI learning. Ensuring **neutral, descriptive labels** instead of **stereotypical or gendered labels** can make a significant difference.

For example, instead of labeling:

- *"Young Black male with a hoodie"*, use *"Person wearing a hoodie."*
- *"Asian woman working in a store"*, use *"Retail worker at a store."*

3. Implement Bias Detection Pipelines

Bias can creep in at multiple stages of AI development. Using tools like **bias detection dashboards, adversarial testing, and fairness benchmarks** can help detect **hidden biases** before deploying AI models.

One approach is **contrastive testing**, where we compare AI outputs across **different demographic groups** and adjust the model accordingly.

4. Fine-Tune Models for Fairness

Instead of retraining entire models, we can **fine-tune them with fairness-aware objectives**. This involves adjusting **weights** so that outputs remain balanced across diverse inputs.

```python
from transformers import TrainingArguments, Trainer

# Example: Fine-tuning DeepSeek-VL with fairness constraints
training_args = TrainingArguments(
    output_dir="./deepseek-vl-fairness",
    evaluation_strategy="epoch",
    save_total_limit=2,
    per_device_train_batch_size=8,
)

trainer = Trainer(
    model=model,
```

```
        args=training_args,
        train_dataset=fairness_balanced_dataset
)

trainer.train()
```

This method **ensures the model doesn't reinforce existing biases**.

Looking Ahead: The Future of Fair AI

Bias in multimodal AI is a **complex but solvable problem**. Researchers are developing **more advanced fairness-aware training techniques**, such as:

Differential Fairness Learning – Ensuring equal accuracy across demographic groups.
Debiasing with Counterfactual Data – Training AI on *what-if scenarios* to reduce biased associations.
AI Governance & Regulation – Policies ensuring ethical AI development.

The road to **fair and unbiased AI** isn't just about **better technology**—it's about **better human decision-making**. If we approach AI development with **inclusivity, responsibility, and fairness**, we can create multimodal AI that serves **everyone** equally.

8.2 Responsible AI Development

Artificial intelligence is evolving at an incredible pace, but with great power comes great responsibility. The question isn't just about *what AI can do*, but *what it should do*. Responsible AI development isn't just about preventing harm—it's about ensuring AI benefits everyone, fairly and ethically.

When working with models like DeepSeek-VL, which combine **vision and language**, ethical considerations become even more crucial. These models process images and text together, meaning **bias, misinformation, and harmful outputs** can emerge from either modality. So how do we ensure that our AI systems are **transparent, accountable, and beneficial**?

Let's explore the principles of responsible AI development and how to apply them in real-world scenarios.

What is Responsible AI?

Responsible AI refers to designing, developing, and deploying AI systems that align with ethical guidelines, legal frameworks, and human values. This includes principles like:

- **Fairness:** AI should treat all users equitably, regardless of race, gender, or background.
- **Transparency:** Users should understand how AI makes decisions.
- **Accountability:** Developers should take responsibility for AI's actions and impacts.
- **Privacy & Security:** AI should protect user data and prevent misuse.
- **Sustainability:** AI should be designed with efficiency and environmental considerations in mind.

These principles aren't just theoretical—they shape **real-world policies and decisions** that impact businesses, consumers, and society as a whole.

Challenges in Responsible AI Development

While AI offers incredible potential, it also presents several ethical challenges:

1. Bias in Data and Decision-Making

AI models learn from historical data, meaning they inherit both **good and bad** patterns. If past data contains **stereotypes or underrepresentation**, AI can reinforce **unfair biases**.

For example, if a vision-language model like DeepSeek-VL is trained on **Western-centric** datasets, it might describe **cultural elements differently** based on geographic biases. Imagine uploading an image of a traditional African ceremony and getting a **generic caption like "People gathering outdoors"**, while a similar image from Europe might receive a **detailed cultural description**.

To mitigate this, developers must:

- Use **diverse, representative datasets**.

- Regularly **audit model outputs** to detect bias.
- Apply **bias correction techniques** during fine-tuning.

---

2. Misinformation and Hallucinations

One major challenge with AI-generated content is **hallucination**—when a model generates **inaccurate or misleading information**.

For example, if a user asks DeepSeek-VL to describe a historical image and it **fabricates** details, the misinformation could spread. In **medical AI applications**, incorrect descriptions could lead to **misinterpretation of scans or symptoms**, putting lives at risk.

To prevent misinformation:

- **Cross-check outputs** with reliable sources.
- Use **confidence scoring** to indicate uncertainty.
- Implement **human-in-the-loop review systems** for high-risk applications.

Let's run a quick test to see if DeepSeek-VL **hallucinates** details in a historical image:

```python
from transformers import AutoProcessor,
AutoModelForVision2Seq
import torch
from PIL import Image

# Load DeepSeek-VL model
processor =
AutoProcessor.from_pretrained("DeepSeekAI/deepseek-vl")
model =
AutoModelForVision2Seq.from_pretrained("DeepSeekAI/deepseek-vl")

def describe_image(image_path):
    image = Image.open(image_path)
    inputs = processor(images=image, return_tensors="pt")

    with torch.no_grad():
        outputs = model.generate(**inputs)

    return processor.decode(outputs[0],
skip_special_tokens=True)
```

```
# Test with a historical image
caption = describe_image("historical_event.jpg")
print("Generated Caption:", caption)
```

If the model **adds details that aren't in the image**, we know there's a problem. The next step is **fine-tuning with fact-checked datasets** to ensure reliability.

---

3. Privacy and Data Security Risks

Vision-language models process **sensitive data**—including images of people, medical records, and personal documents. If AI systems aren't designed with **privacy-first principles**, they can expose **confidential information**.

Some key risks include:

- **Facial recognition misuse** leading to surveillance concerns.
- **Unintended leaks** of personally identifiable information (PII).
- **Malicious use** of AI-generated images for deepfakes.

To mitigate these risks:

- Implement **strong encryption** for AI-generated data.
- Use **differential privacy** techniques to prevent exposure of individual data points.
- Set **clear guidelines** on ethical AI use, especially in sensitive domains like healthcare and finance.

For example, here's how to **remove personally identifiable information (PII)** from AI-generated captions before displaying them:

```python
----
import re

def remove_sensitive_info(caption):
    # Simple regex-based filtering for names, locations, and
numbers
    caption = re.sub(r"\b[A-Z][a-z]+ [A-Z][a-z]+\b",
"[REDACTED]", caption)  # Remove full names
    caption = re.sub(r"\d{4}", "[REDACTED]", caption)  #
Remove years (e.g., birth years)
```

```
    caption = re.sub(r"([A-Z][a-z]+,? [A-Z]{2})",
"[REDACTED]", caption)  # Remove city/state references
    return caption

# Example caption with PII
caption = "John Doe, a doctor in New York, was born in 1985."
print("Filtered Caption:", remove_sensitive_info(caption))
```

This helps prevent **AI-generated content from accidentally exposing user data**.

Building a Responsible AI Development Framework

Ensuring responsible AI isn't just about **one-time fixes**—it requires an **ongoing commitment** to ethical practices. Here's how teams can integrate responsibility into their AI workflow:

Step 1: Ethical Dataset Curation

- Source **diverse, unbiased datasets** from multiple regions and demographics.
- Regularly **audit and refine** datasets to remove harmful patterns.
- Use **synthetic data augmentation** to balance representation.

Step 2: Fairness-Optimized Model Training

- Apply **bias mitigation techniques** such as adversarial debiasing.
- Train with **fairness constraints** to prevent discrimination.
- Conduct **robust testing** across different demographic groups.

Step 3: Transparent Model Behavior

- Provide **explanations for AI decisions** using explainable AI (XAI) techniques.
- Use **confidence scores** to indicate uncertainty in model outputs.
- Offer **user controls** for adjusting model behavior.

Step 4: Ethical Deployment and Monitoring

- Conduct **regular audits** of deployed AI models.
- Implement **automated bias detection dashboards**.
- Allow **user feedback loops** to report unfair or harmful outputs.

By embedding these principles into AI development, we can ensure that **vision-language models like DeepSeek-VL are not just powerful, but also ethical, reliable, and aligned with human values**.

Final Thoughts: The Road Ahead

The future of AI isn't just about making models smarter—it's about making them **safer, fairer, and more accountable**. Responsible AI isn't a **one-time task**; it's an **ongoing process** that requires vigilance, adaptation, and commitment from researchers, developers, and policymakers alike.

With a balanced approach—combining **technical safeguards, ethical oversight, and continuous improvement**—we can build AI that truly serves humanity.

The goal isn't just to create AI that works. The goal is to create AI that works for everyone.

8.3 Future Advancements and Research Directions

The world of vision-language AI is evolving rapidly, and models like **DeepSeek-VL** are just the beginning. As researchers push boundaries, new advancements will shape the way we interact with multimodal AI, unlocking capabilities that were once confined to science fiction. But where is the field headed? What breakthroughs can we expect in the coming years?

This chapter explores the future of vision-language AI, from **technical innovations** to **emerging research directions** that could redefine human-AI interaction.

The Next Generation of Vision-Language Models

Today's models, while impressive, still have limitations. **They struggle with nuanced reasoning, suffer from biases, and occasionally hallucinate incorrect information.** The next generation of AI will focus on solving these challenges while introducing entirely new capabilities.

1. Unified Multimodal Learning

Current vision-language models are trained to **understand and generate text from images** or **retrieve relevant images from text queries**. However, future systems will take this a step further by **seamlessly integrating multiple data types** beyond just images and text.

Imagine an AI that can:

- Analyze **videos** in real-time and provide live captions, context, and analysis.
- Process **3D spatial data** to understand the real world, unlocking applications in robotics and AR/VR.
- Incorporate **audio and sensor data**, enabling AI assistants that can interpret human emotion and environmental cues.

2. Continual and Self-Supervised Learning

Most AI models today are **trained once and frozen**, meaning they don't improve without additional retraining. But researchers are working on **continual learning**, where AI can:

- Learn **incrementally from new data** without forgetting previous knowledge.
- Adapt to **real-world changes** without expensive retraining.
- Improve through **self-supervised techniques**, using raw, unstructured data rather than relying on labeled datasets.

One exciting direction is **self-learning multimodal models**, which can refine their understanding over time by interacting with users. Instead of being purely passive, future AI could **ask clarifying questions**, seek feedback, and improve based on experience.

Bridging the Gap Between Perception and Reasoning

One of the biggest challenges in multimodal AI today is **deep reasoning**. Models like DeepSeek-VL can generate image captions and answer visual questions, but they don't yet possess **true comprehension**.

For example, if shown a picture of a broken bridge and asked, "What will happen if a car tries to cross this bridge?" most models would struggle to provide a **logical answer**. They recognize objects but fail to **predict consequences**.

Future AI will integrate **common-sense reasoning and physics-based understanding**, allowing for:

- **Causal inference**, where AI can predict outcomes based on visual and textual inputs.
- **Spatial awareness**, enabling applications in robotics, self-driving cars, and augmented reality.
- **Abstract thinking**, where AI can understand metaphorical and non-literal visual contexts.

One promising research area is **neuro-symbolic AI**, which combines **deep learning with symbolic reasoning** to create AI that can not only recognize patterns but also logically deduce new information.

The Role of Multimodal AI in Emerging Technologies

1. Human-AI Collaboration

Instead of just being **assistive tools**, future multimodal models will act as **true collaborators** in creative and technical fields. Imagine:

- AI-generated **mood boards** for artists, where the model suggests designs based on textual prompts and real-world images.
- AI **coding assistants** that interpret diagrams and handwritten notes to generate working software.
- AI-powered **scientific discovery**, where models analyze complex visual data to suggest new hypotheses.

These advancements will redefine the **human-AI relationship**, making machines **partners rather than passive tools**.

2. Real-Time AI for Augmented and Virtual Reality

AR and VR are **natural fits** for vision-language AI. In the near future, we might see:

- **Real-time scene understanding**, where AI overlays information on objects in the real world.

- **AI-powered accessibility tools**, such as smart glasses that describe surroundings for visually impaired users.
- **Intelligent AR assistants**, helping engineers troubleshoot complex systems by analyzing visual inputs.

Companies like **Apple, Meta, and Google** are already investing heavily in this space, and multimodal AI will be a **core technology** driving next-generation experiences.

3. AI That Understands Human Emotion

One of the most exciting frontiers is **affective AI**—models that can **read and respond to human emotions** based on facial expressions, tone of voice, and contextual cues.

- **Healthcare applications:** AI assistants detecting early signs of depression or anxiety based on facial cues and speech patterns.
- **Personalized learning:** AI tutors adjusting their teaching style based on a student's emotional state.
- **Customer support:** AI chatbots recognizing frustration and responding with empathy.

These advancements raise **ethical concerns**—how much emotional intelligence should AI possess? And how do we prevent misuse? Researchers will need to navigate these questions carefully.

The Road Ahead: Challenges and Open Questions

Despite the exciting progress, **multimodal AI still has major hurdles to overcome**.

1. Ethical and Bias Issues

As AI becomes more integrated into daily life, **bias, misinformation, and security risks** become even more significant. Researchers must:

- Develop **fairer training datasets** that represent diverse cultures and perspectives.
- Create **explainable AI models** that provide transparency into their decision-making.

- Implement **stronger safeguards** against misuse, such as deepfake detection and misinformation filtering.

2. Computational Costs and Sustainability

Training massive vision-language models requires enormous computing power, leading to concerns about **energy consumption and environmental impact**. Future AI research will focus on:

- **More efficient architectures** that require less computation.
- **Low-power AI models** optimized for edge devices and mobile applications.
- **Sustainable AI practices** that reduce the carbon footprint of AI training and inference.

3. The Limits of AI Understanding

Can AI ever truly **"understand"** the world as humans do? While future models will become **better at reasoning, prediction, and creativity**, fundamental questions remain:

- Will AI ever develop **true consciousness**?
- Can AI **learn** in a way that mimics human cognition?
- Where should we **draw the line** between AI assistance and AI autonomy?

These questions are at the heart of **AI ethics, philosophy, and long-term research**.

Final Thoughts: The Future is Multimodal

The future of AI isn't just about **text-based models like ChatGPT or image generators like Stable Diffusion**—it's about creating **seamless, multimodal systems** that combine **vision, language, sound, and action** into one unified intelligence.

DeepSeek-VL is an early glimpse of this future, but what comes next will be even more **transformative**. Whether it's **AI-powered AR assistants, real-time emotional AI, or reasoning-driven models**, the next decade will redefine the way humans and AI interact.

We're not just building smarter AI—we're building AI that sees, thinks, and understands the world alongside us.

www.ingramcontent.com/pod-product-compliance
Lightning Source LLC
LaVergne TN
LVHW080118070326
832902LV00015B/2647